EDITOR: LEE JOHNSO

## ELITE SERI
# US MARINE CORPS 1941-45

*Text by*
GORDON ROTTMAN
*Colour plates by*
MIKE CHAPPELL

First published in Great Britain in 1995 by
Osprey, a division of Reed Consumer Books Ltd.
Michelin House, 81 Fulham Road,
London SW3 6RB
and Auckland, Melbourne, Singapore and Toronto.

© Copyright 1995 Reed International Books Ltd.
Reprinted 1997 (twice)

All rights reserved. Apart from any fair dealing for the purpose of private study, research, criticism or review, as permitted under the Copyright Designs and Patents Act, 1988, no part of this publication may be reproduced, stored in a retrieval system, or transmitted in any form or by any means, electronic, electrical, chemical, mechanical, optical, photocopying, recording or otherwise, without the prior permission of the copyright owner. Enquiries should be addressed to the Publishers.

ISBN 1 85532 497 0

Filmset in Great Britain by Keyspools Ltd.
Printed through World Print Ltd, Hong Kong

## Acknowledgments
The author is sincerely grateful to David Bingham (Curator, Ft Polk Museum) for the use of his extensive library; Major Charles Melson, USMC (Ret) for his expert advice; Shelby Stanton; Ron Volstad; Beauragard Parish Interlibrary Loan Service; Ft Polk Library; and the former Marines who enriched this book by providing uniform, weapon and equipment slang terms. Unless otherwise stated, all photos are from US Marine Corps and US Navy sources.

For a catalogue of all books published by Osprey Military please write to:
Osprey Direct, 27 Sanders Road,
Wellington NN8 4NL

## Author's note
The following abbreviations have been used in this book:

| | |
|---|---|
| Amtrac | Amphibian Tractor |
| Arty | Artillery |
| AT | Antitank |
| BAR | Browning Automatic Rifle |
| Bn | Battalion |
| CB | Construction Battalion ('Seabees') |
| Co | Company |
| Engr | Engineer |
| FMFPac | Fleet Marine Force, Pacific |
| HBT | Herringbone Twill |
| IIIAC | III Amphibious Corps |
| IMAC | I Marine Amphibious Corps |
| Med | Medical |
| MT | Motor Transport |
| OD | Olive Drab |
| PhibCorpsPacFlt | Amphibious Corps, Pacific Fleet |
| Pio | Pioneer |
| Regt | Regiment |
| Spl Wpns | Special Weapons |
| Svc | Service |
| USMC | United States Marine Corps |
| USMCR | United States Marine Corps Reserve |
| USMCWR | United States Marine Corps Women's Reserve |
| VAC | V Amphibious Corps |

## Publisher's note
Readers may wish to study this title in conjunction with the following Osprey publications:

| | |
|---|---|
| MAA 70 | *The US Army 1941–45* |
| MAA 205 | *US Army Combat Equipments* |
| Elite 2 | *The US Marine Corps since 1945* |
| Elite 43 | *Vietnam Marines 1965–73* |
| Elite 55 | *Marine Recon 1940–90* |
| Campaign 18 | *Guadalcanal 1942* |

## Artist's note
Readers may care to note that the original paintings from which the colour plates in this book were prepared are available for private sale. All reproduction copyright whatsoever is retained by the publisher.

All enquiries should be addressed to:

Mike Chappell
14 Downlands
Walmer
Deal
Kent CT14 7XA

The publishers regret that they can enter into no correspondence upon this matter.

# US MARINE CORPS 1941–45

## INTRODUCTION

While the US Marine Corps was one of the smallest of American armed services in World War II (only the Coast Guard was smaller), its contribution to the final victory cannot be overstated. The Marines comprised a mere 5 per cent of America's 16.3 million men and women in uniform, but suffered 10 per cent of the nation's combat casualties.

On average, among all US armed forces, 73 per cent served overseas, but in the Marine Corps 98 per cent of its officers and 89 per cent of its enlisted men had been deployed abroad by the end of the war. While the Army conducted many more, and sometimes larger, amphibious assaults, the Marines conducted proportionally more. In the Pacific, 18 Army divisions executed 26 landings, compared to 15 by six Marine divisions; these landings were often followed by some of the most brutal combat experienced by US forces. The price of victory was high: the Corps suffered 19,733 dead and missing and 67,207 wounded out of a total of 669,000 who wore the Marine uniform.

At the war's beginning the Corps possessed 65,881 officers and men: just over 31,000 belonged to the Fleet Marine Force's ground and air units; some 3,400 guarded overseas naval bases; almost 4,000 served aboard ships of the fleet; and 27,000 manned the shore establishment and guarded Stateside naval bases. By the war's end there were 485,833 men and women in the Marines, and to place this expansion in perspective, more Marines were wounded in action through 46 months of combat than the Corps had originally possessed on 7 December 1941. Interestingly, over 224,000 conscripts were inducted into the Corps, which prior to 1943 had been solely a volunteer force, and all but 70,000 draftees volunteered to become regulars or active reservists. Although the US Marine Corps is a component of the Navy, it operates autonomously. While its most notable achievements were those of the Fleet Marine Force ground and air combat units, the Marines maintained their earliest role, as that of ships' detachments and naval base guards.

It must be remembered that the Marine Corps is a self-contained fighting force and possesses its own air component. There is not enough room here to cover Marine aviation, but it is nonetheless a major component of the Corps. At the outbreak of hostilities, Marine aviation possessed only 251 aircraft and 2,766 men (of whom just over 600 were pilots). By 1945 the fledgling air arm had grown to 32 aircraft groups and 145 squadrons, with 125,162 personnel; it accounted for 2,355 Japanese aircraft destroyed in air combat.

Regardless of facts and figures, one single message prevails: whether called a leatherneck, sea soldier or gyrene, it was the individual Marine and his rifle that made the Corps what it remains to this day, one of the world's elite fighting forces.

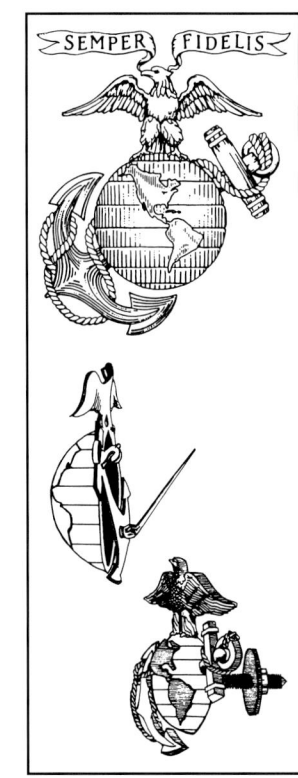

*The US Marine Corps 'globe and anchor', or 'chicken on a ball', device was standardised on 16 March 1936 as a cap and collar ornament. It was incorporated into a variety of insignia and borne on unit colours, Its basic design was In use since 1868 and was influenced by the Royal Marine's badge. Officers wore a silver globe with gilt continents and gilt anchor with silver rope for blues while enlisted men's were brass. Bronze devices were worn on forest green and khaki uniforms by all ranks. The scroll (not included on uniform insignia) bore 'SEMPER FIDELIS' – 'Always Faithful', the Marine Corps' motto. Beneath are the two types of fasteners in use during World War II, pin and screw.*

# MARINE ORGANISATION

It has long been said that the Marines deploy as brigades but fight as divisions. The five brigades formed just prior to, during, and immediately after the war were tied directly to specific divisions. They were raised for a specific purpose, usually a rapid deployment. Only one saw combat and in itself became a division. The division was the basic combat formation assigned the task of executing major amphibious assaults and securing island objectives.

The largest permanent Marine formations prior to early 1941 were the 1st and 2nd Marine Brigades, formed on the East and West Coasts in 1935–36. Each brigade was built around an infantry regiment and an aircraft group, but all units were nevertheless under strength. If deployed for combat, it was planned to supplement them with ships' guards. Initially, the Fleet Marine Force (FMF) was oriented principally toward the Atlantic and Caribbean; the Pacific at that time was of secondary importance. From 1940–41 German submarines were the major threat, and the fear that Germany might occupy French possessions in the Caribbean and possibly attack the Azores. It was not until the summer of 1941 that the FMF began to focus its attention more on the Pacific. By that time the entire 15,000-man Marine Corps Reserve had been mobilised and the Marine Corps itself consisted of some 50,000 troops, though its units were still largely under strength.

### Marine division organisation

The forming of Marine divisions was proposed in 1940. The new 1st and 2nd Marine Divisions (MarDiv) were formed in early 1941 by converting the two permanent brigades. They were slow in developing, and it was not until mid-1942 that they were considered ready for deployment. By then they had matured into a standard structure with sufficiently diverse units to make them self-contained amphibious fighting forces well suited for combat on rugged tropical islands.

Several changes were introduced each year of the war to capitalise on lessons learned from previous operations, to adapt to expected Japanese resistance, increase firepower, reduce manpower needs, provide for more effective allocation of resources between divisions and corps, and to further streamline divisional logistics. The few units deleted from the division were reassigned to the FMF. (Unlike the Army's divisions, which have endured many and varied reorganisations, today's Marine division bears a striking resemblance to its World War II predecessor. Even the assignment of regiments has changed little.) In 1941 each division consisted of a division headquarters; service, medical, engineer, light tank and parachute battalions; scout, anti-aircraft machine

*A 1st MarDiv weapons platoon, armed with M1919A4 machine guns, undertakes landing training on Chesapeake Bay in early 1942. At this time the Marines were still planning to participate in the invasion of North Africa alongside the Army. (Shelby Stanton collection)*

gun, signal, chemical, guard and motor transport companies; two infantry regiments; and an artillery regiment.

Ongoing fleet landing exercises identified numerous flaws in unit organisation, equipment, logistical support and tactics. As a result a pioneer battalion was added, to provide manpower for moving supplies from landing beaches to combat units. This new unit, along with the existing engineer battalion, and an attached naval construction battalion[1] were placed in a new engineer regiment. A headquarters battalion was formed to consolidate divisional command and to control the various elements. The anti-aircraft company was absorbed into a new special weapons battalion, along with new anti-tank sub-units. A third infantry regiment was added, along with amphibian tractor, service, and medical battalions, while the chemical company was deleted. The concept of 'triangular reinforcement' was strictly adhered to by the Marines. Divisional combat support and service units were organised for attachment to the three regiments and this concept was applied at all lower levels. The division headquarters battalion had headquarters, signal and military police companies. A reconnaissance company was added in 1944.

The infantry regiment was the core of the division's fighting force. While its basic organisation changed little over the war years, its allocation of manpower and weapons did, and it underwent refinements in sub-unit organisation. Command and control, and minimal service support was provided by a headquarters and service company. A regimental weapons company had three 37 mm gun platoons (4×37 mm AT; 20 mm AA/AT guns prior to 1943) and a 75 mm gun platoon (2×75 mm M3 self-propelled AT guns, 4 in 1944).

Each of the three infantry battalions had a headquarters company, three rifle companies, and a weapons company (until 1944). The rifle companies had a large headquarters element, three rifle platoons and a weapons platoon, which after May 1944 was replaced by a machine gun platoon. Rifle platoons numbered between 42 and 46 men. The platoon headquarters had a 2nd lieutenant platoon leader, platoon sergeant, and five radio operators and messengers. Prior to 1944 they had three nine-man rifle squads consisting of a squad leader (sergeant), assistant squad leader (corporal), two scouts, three riflemen (all armed with M1 rifles), a grenadier (M1 rifle, M7 rifle grenade launcher or, prior to 1943, M1903 rifle, M1 grenade launcher), and an automatic rifle man (M1918A2BAR). The automatic rifle squad had a squad leader (M50 sub-machine gun), two automatic riflemen, and five riflemen. From April 1943, some riflemen were redesignated assistant automatic riflemen and armed with M1 carbines.

However, there was an alternative squad organisation in the works. Early in the 1927–33 Nicaraguan

[1] More commonly known as 'Seabees', derived from 'CB' for Construction Battalions.

### Division, Regiment, and Battalion Strengths

| YEAR | MARDIV | INF REGT | INF BN |
|---|---|---|---|
| 1942 | 19,514 | 3,168 | 933 |
| 1943 | 19,965 | 3,242 | 953 |
| 1944–45 | 17,465 | 3,218 | 918 |

(strength includes assigned Navy personnel)

### Provisional Marine Brigade Orders of Battle, 1941–47

| MARINE BRIGADE | DEPLOYMENT LOCATION | INF REGT(S) | ARTILLERY BATTALION(S) | DEFENSE BATTALION(S) |
|---|---|---|---|---|
| 1st (41–42) | Iceland | 6 | 2/10 | 5(–) |
| 2nd (41–43) | Amer Samoa | 8(3)[1] | 1/10 (3/12[2]) | 2, 7 |
| 3rd (42–43) | West Samoa | 7 | 1/11 | 2, 5, 7, 8 |
| Tac Gp 1 (44) | Eniwetok | 22,106[3] | 22 Pack How | 10 |
| Task Gp A (44) | Emirau | 4 | 4 Pack How | 14 |
| 1st (44) | Guam | 4,22,305[4] | 4, 22 Pack How | – |
| 3rd (46–47) | North China | 4 | 3/12 | – |

Remarks: 1. Replaced 8th Marines in September 1942. 2. Replaced 1st Bn, 10th Marines in September 1942. 3. Army 106th Inf Regt, 27th Inf Div. 4. Army 305th Inf Regt, 77th Inf Div.

Campaign Lt. Merritt Edson of the 5th Marines had developed the technique of dividing rifle units into three- and four-man 'fighting groups' centred around an automatic weapon. This had proved extremely successful for jungle patrols. Later, when Major Edson and other 4th Marines officers examined the concept, by then known as 'fighting teams', in China in the late 1930s, and the 1st and 2nd Raider Battalions (Lt.Col. Edson commanded the 1st) organised their squads under this concept in 1941. It was also tried out by the 22nd Marines at Eniwetok in early 1944, and was credited with enabling small-unit leaders to continue their missions when communication was lost and the unit was under heavy fire. The new 4th Marines, formed from the raider battalions, continued the technique. Reports by these and other units led the headquarters of the Marine Corps to test the concept seriously in the States using the 24th Marines. By the end of March 1944 the rifle company table of organisation had been changed to reflect the use of four-man 'fire teams' and the automatic rifle squad was dissolved.

The new rifle squad organisation called for a squad leader (sergeant; M1 carbine) leading three fire teams composed of a team leader (corporal; M1 rifle, M7 grenade launcher), rifleman (M1 rifle, M7 grenade launcher), automatic rifleman (M1918A2 BAR) and assistant automatic rifleman (M1 carbine). The four-man fire teams allowed the triangular organisation concept to be maintained down to the smallest tactical entity, with every commander or leader controlling three manoeuvre elements, be it regiments, battalions, companies, platoons, squads, teams or men. Additionally, 27 each of 2.36 in. bazookas, flamethrowers and demolition kits – one per rifle squad – were pooled in the battalion headquarters.

The rifle company's weapons platoon had a small headquarters as well as machine gun and mortar sections. To begin with they had two .30-cal. M1919A4 light machine guns and two 60 mm mortars. This was increased to five machine guns and three mortars in April 1943. The weapons platoon was redesignated a machine gun platoon in May 1944, with six M1919A4 light and six M1917A1 heavy machine guns; the latter transferred from the by then disbanded battalion weapons company. The

### Marine Division Orders of Battle, 1941–47

| MARINE DIVISION | INF REGTS | ARTY REGT | ENGINEER UNITS[1] | TANK BN | SPECIAL TROOPS SPL WPNS BN | SERVICE TROOPS | RECON CO | SVC BN | MED BN | MT BN | AMTRAC BN |
|---|---|---|---|---|---|---|---|---|---|---|---|
| 1st (41–44) | 1, 5, 7 | 11 | 17 Regt[2] | 1 | 1 | | – | 1 | 1 | – | 1 |
| 1st (44–47) | 1, 5, 7 | 11 | 1 Engr, 1 Pio | 1 | – | | 1 | 1 | 1 | 1 | – |
| 2d (41–44) | 2, 6, 8, 9[3] | 10 | 18 Regt[4] | 2 | 2 | 2AT[5] | – | 2 | 2 | – | 2 |
| 2d (44–47) | 2, 6, 8 | 10 | 2 Engr, 2 Pio | 2 | – | | 2 | 2 | 2 | 2 | – |
| 3d (42–44) | 3[6], 9, 21 | 12[7] | 19 Regt[8] | 3 | 3 | | – | 3 | 3 | – | 3 |
| 3d (44–45) | 3, 9, 21 | 12 | 3 Eng, 3 Pio | 3 | – | | 3 | 3 | 3 | 3 | – |
| 4th (42–44) | 23, 24, 25 | 14 | 20 Regt[9] | 4 | 4 | | – | 4 | 4 | – | 4 |
| 4th (44–45) | 23, 24, 25 | 14 | 4 Engr, 4 Pio | 4 | – | | 4 | 4 | 4 | 4 | – |
| 5th (44) | 26, 27, 28 | 13 | 16 Regt[10] | 5 | 5 | | – | 5 | 5 | – | 5 |
| 5th (44–46) | 26, 27, 28 | 13 | 5 Engr, 5 Pio | 5 | – | | 5 | 5 | 5 | 5 | – |
| 6th (44–46) | 4, 22, 29 | 15 | 6 Engr, 6 Pio | 6 | – | | 6 | 6 | 6 | 6 | – |

Remarks:
1. Divisional engineer regiments included the engineer and pioneer battalions listed beneath it as its 1st and 2nd Bns respectively, plus a naval const battalion as its 3rd Bn.
2. Deleted in the May 1944 reorganization. Never assigned a naval const battalion.
3. The newly formed 9th Marines was attached to 2nd MarDiv February 1942 until reassigned to 3rd MarDiv September 1943.
4. Its 3rd Bn was 18th Naval Const Bn. Deleted in May 1944 reorganization, but 1st MarDiv embarked prior to this date and it was retained until August 1944 for the Saipan/Tinian operation.
5. The 2nd Anti tank Bn was assigned to 2nd MarDiv in 1943 only.
6. The newly formed 3rd Marines joined 3rd MarDiv in June 1943 to replace 23rd Marines, still in the States and later assigned to 4th MarDiv.
7. The 12th Marines was not assigned until February 1943.
8. Its 3rd Bn was 25th Naval Const Bn. Deleted in May 1944 reorganization, but 3rd MarDiv embarked prior to this date and it was retained until September 1944 for the Guam operation.
9. Its 3rd Bn was 121st Naval Const Bn. Deleted in May 1944 reorganization, but 4th MarDiv embarked prior to this date and it was retained until August 1944 for the Saipan/Tinian operation.
10. Deactivated in May 1944 before overseas deployment.

weapons platoon's 60 mm mortar section was transferred to the company headquarters.

The battalion weapons company began with an anti-aircraft and anti-tank gun platoon (4×20 mm AA/AT), mortar platoon (4×81 mm) and three machine gun platoons (8×M1917A1 each). In April 1943 the anti-tank platoon was deleted and the machine gun platoons were reduced to four M1917A1s each. The battalion weapons company was dissolved in May 1944, with the three machine gun platoons' assets transferred to the rifle companies and the 81 mm mortar platoon moved to the battalion headquarters company.

The May 1944 reorganisation (i.e. deletion of the battalion weapons company and rifle company weapons platoon, reallocation of crew-served weapons to the more immediate user level, and institution of the fire team) allowed for more effective combat organisation, efficient weapons employment and tactical teamwork. (The reorganisation had been announced in January 1944 and the 2nd and 4th MarDivs soon began reorganising. They completed it in May and assaulted Saipan in June. The other divisions were reorganised in time for their subsequent operations.)

The Marines occasionally utilised separate infantry regiments for special deployments. These included the 3rd, 4th, 9th, 21st, 22nd and 24th Marines (Reinforced), either detached from divisions or as actual separate units. They were usually reinforced with a 75 mm pack howitzer battalion and tank, engineer, pioneer, signal, motor transport, and medical companies plus service detachments to make them self-sufficient.

The artillery regiment went through several reorganisations that changed the number of battalions and the calibres of assigned weapons. Prior to 1943 there were three 75 mm howitzer battalions and one of 105 mm. This was changed to three 75 mm and two 105 mm battalions in April 1943. In May 1944 one 75 mm battalion was converted to 165 mm. In late 1945 the 75 mm pack howitzers were withdrawn, leaving one 155 mm and three 105 mm

*Above: 1st MarDiv Marines embark a troop train bound for the West Coast, 1942. They wear khakis, without leggings, new M1 steel helmets, and M1941 field gear in the field transport pack configuration.*

*Left: Marines debark from a troop train while being transferred from the East to West Coast, 1942. All wear forest green winter service uniforms and are armed with the M1903 Springfield. (Shelby Stanton collection)*

howitzer battalions. The 105 mm batteries had four pieces, until 1943 when they received two more, while the 75 mm batteries had six from the beginning. The regiment and battalions each had a headquarters and service battery.

The engineer regiments possessed engineer, pioneer and naval construction battalions, each with a headquarters and three 'line' companies. While officially dissolved in May 1944, the 2nd, 3rd, and 4th MarDivs had embarked for combat operations prior to this, and their regiments were retained at least through August.

The old division tank companies were redesignated scout companies in early 1941. They had 14 M3A1 scout cars and motorcycles. The companies were incorporated into the new light tank battalions raised in late 1941, but retained their original designations – 1st and 2nd. The four tank companies had 18 M3-series tanks (three platoons of five and three in the headquarters). The scout cars and motorcycles were never employed in combat; the scout companies normally patrolled on foot. In April 1943 battalions lost a company to newly forming divisions and the scouts were usually redesignated Company D. In May 1944 the battalions were authorised M4-series tanks and 'light' was dropped from their designation. Each company had 15 tanks – four per platoon and three in the headquarters. The battalions were not immediately and completely re-equipped with medium tanks. Some were committed to combat with one or two medium tank companies and the rest were equipped with light tanks. At the same time, the scout companies were redesignated reconnaissance, assigned their parent division's number, and reassigned to the division headquarters battalion.

The special weapons battalion originally had two

Marine raiders cross a bridge constructed of linked toggle ropes, a technique borrowed from the British Commandos. Carried by each raider, these consisted of an 8 ft. rope with a loop on one end and a wood handle on the other. Outfitted in camouflage utilities, they are armed with M1903 rifles. (Shelby Stanton collection)

anti-aircraft artillery batteries (one with 16×40 mm, the other with 6×90 mm guns) and three anti-tank batteries (each with 6×37 mm and 2×75 mm self-propelled AT guns). In April 1943 the 90 mm battery was deleted. The battalion was dissolved in May 1944; the 75 mm self-propelled guns were reassigned to regimental weapons companies, and the 40 mm guns to the new anti-aircraft battalions.

Divisional service troops had three types of battalions. The service battalion originally had headquarters, service and supply, ordnance, one division and three regimental transport companies. In 1943 a motor transport battalion was added and the transport companies were transferred to it and restructured into three companies. The medical battalion's five companies were manned mainly by Navy medical personnel (surgeons, dentists, corpsmen and technicians), but something over one-fifth of its strength was Marine support personnel. From late 1943 to 1945 the 1st to 4th MarDivs consolidated their division headquarters and service battalions into a single headquarters and service battalion.

The amphibian tractor battalion, a component of the service troops, had 100 standard amtracs and 59

Troops of the 1st Raider Battalion practise landing from a Landing Craft, Rubber (Large) (LCR(L)) at Camp Lejeune, N.C. The foremost raider carries a Reising M50 submachine gun.

support amtracs divided between its headquarters and service company and three tractor companies. In 1943 the number of support amtracs was increased to 73. The battalion was removed from the division in 1944, but that did not signal the end of organic amtracs, since engineer, pioneer, and motor transport battalions were still equipped with a total of 71 specialised support amtracs.

### Fleet Marine Force units

The FMF possessed a pool of combat support and service units for attachment to amphibious corps and Marine divisions, or for special employment. The principal units are discussed here; others are addressed in the Marine Units section.

Each 503-man parachute battalion was originally composed of a headquarters company and companies A, B, and C. When the 1st Parachute Regiment was formed in 1943, the companies were redesignated in sequence through the regiment's battalions: 1st – A, B, C; 2nd – E, F, G; 3rd – I, K, L; and 4th – N, O, P. Companies D, H, M and Q were reserved, in the event of battalion weapons companies being authorised. The rifle companies had three rifle platoons, each armed with a 2.36 in. bazooka, a 60 mm mortar, and three M1941 light machine guns. The Regiment possessed a headquarters and service company and a weapons company.

Prior to the formation of the 1st Raider Regi-

*Artillery men practise loading a 75 mm M1A1 pack howitzer aboard a Landing Craft, Vehicle, Personnel (LCVP) at New River, N.C. They wear their M1941 gear in the field marching pack configuration.*

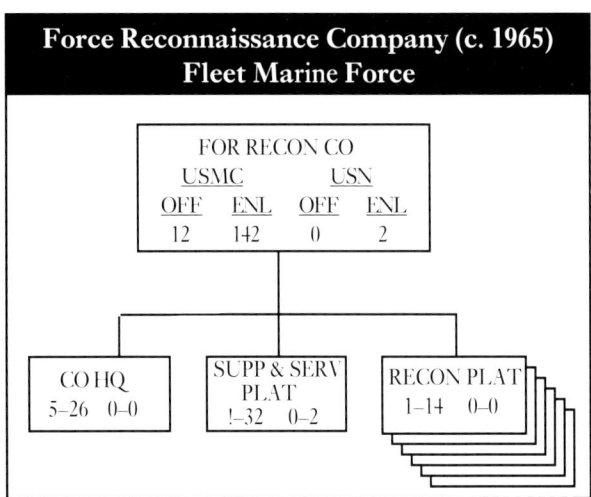

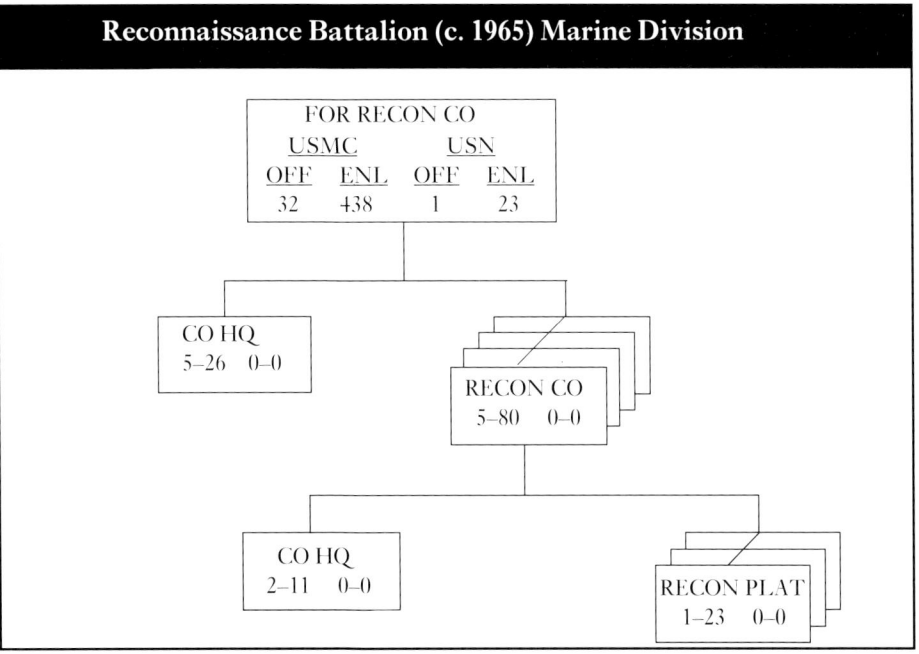

Companies H, M and Q were weapons. This system remained in effect even when the 2nd and 3rd Raider Battalions were attached to the 2nd Raider Regiment (Provisional). The rifle companies had a weapons and three rifle platoons each with three nine-man squads. The weapons platoon had two each of M1919A4 machine guns, .55-cal. anti-tank rifles and 60 mm mortars. The weapons company had a demolitions ($2 \times$ .55-cal. AT rifles), a mortar ($3 \times 60$ mm) and two machine gun ($4 \times$ M1919A4) platoons.

The defence battalions' structure varied a great deal, since they were organised to perform specific missions (in the early days they were often split between islands, and detachments from one battalion could reinforce another), and it was not uncommon for additional provisional batteries to be formed. The 6th Defense Battalion (Reinforced) on Midway Island in June 1942 had a total of seven coast defence and eight anti-aircraft batteries. The battalions were virtually of regimental size. From 1939 to 1943 they

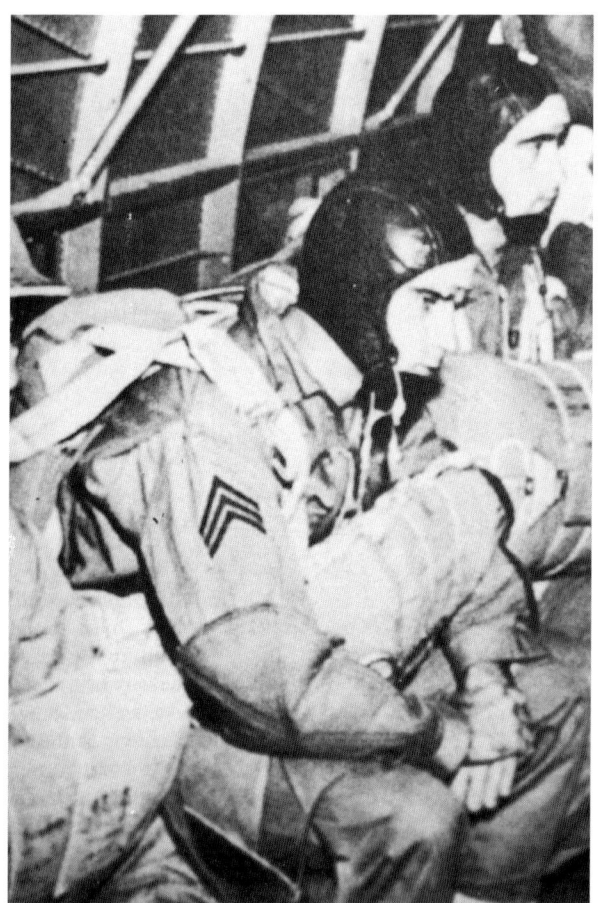

*Above: 'Paramarines' await the green light aboard an R4D-1 (same as Army Air Forces C-47), 1942. This sergeant wears forest green on khaki chevrons on sage green parachutist coveralls. His headgear is a seal brown leather A-7 summer flying helmet.*

*Left: A Marine parachutist prepares to board his aircraft wearing an M1 steel helmet, without a liner, over a seal brown leather A-7 summer flying helmet with sage green parachutist coveralls. He is outfitted with a Navy NAF 68514 troop parachute.*

ment in 1943, battalions had a weapons company and four rifle companies designated A, B, C, D (rifle) and E (weapons). For a time the 2nd Raider Battalion had companies A to F (all rifle). The 4th Raider Battalion initially had only companies A to C (rifle) and D (weapons); between December 1942 and February 1943 it had companies A to D (rifle), E (demolitions) and F (engineer); it was then reorganised as the other battalions. Upon formation of the 1st Raider Regiment, the battalions were reorganised with a weapons company and three rifle companies, designated in sequence through the regiment: 1st – A, B, C, D; 2nd – E, F, G, H; 3rd – I, K, L, M; and 4th – N, O, P, Q.

generally consisted of a coast defence group with three coast defence gun batteries (usually 5 in. guns), an anti-aircraft group with a searchlight and three anti-aircraft gun batteries (4× 3 in. AA guns), and a machine gun group with two batteries (one with .50-cal. water-cooled for AA, the other with M1917A1s for beach defence). From 1943 to 1944 they had a 155 mm artillery group with two batteries (4× 155 mm guns), a 90 mm anti-aircraft group with a searchlight and four gun batteries (4× 90 mm), and a special weapons group (sometimes referred to as a light anti-aircraft group) with three batteries (two with 18× 40 mm, one with 18× 20 mm). The battalion and groups each had headquarters and service batteries, and there was usually a light tank platoon. The battalions were also equipped with SCR-268 early warning radars and sound locators.

The defence battalions were converted to anti-aircraft artillery battalions between April and September 1944, and their artillery groups formed the core of new artillery battalions. The AAA battalions consisted of heavy and light AAA groups; the former had three batteries of 90 mm guns and the latter had three of 40 mm guns, plus a searchlight battery.

The artillery battalions, formed during 1944, had a headquarters and service battery, and three 155 mm howitzer or gun batteries with four pieces each. The 4th Artillery Battalion was equipped with 105 mm howitzers until early 1945.

### Organisation for combat

When task organised for combat, Marine divisions attached combat support and service units down to regimental, battalion and even company level. Typical attachments from the FMF to a division for an assault landing included a war dog platoon, signal intelligence platoon (radio direction finding), provisional rocket detachment (4.5 in. barrage rockets), joint assault signal company (Navy, Marine and Army personnel coordinating naval gunfire, artillery and air support), and amphibian truck company (Ducks), all of which were incorporated in the division after the war. Various artillery, defence and amphibian tractor battalions were also attached, as and when the operation required. Task organised and reinforced regiments were initially called 'combat groups', and their reinforced battalions were called 'combat teams'. In late 1943 these were

*Navy Construction Battalion (CB, or 'Seabees') personnel at Camp Peary, Va., debark from 30 ft. rampless Landing Craft, Personnels with bangalor torpedoes and demolition materials. The Seabee insignia is painted on the LCP's bow. The M1903 rifle armed Seabees wear M1 helmets, one-piece mechanic's coveralls, and leggings.*

redesignated 'regimental landing teams' and 'battalion landing teams' respectively.

For the August 1943 landing on Guadalcanal, the 1st MarDiv formed Combat Groups A (5th Marines) and B (1st Marines). The groups consisted of an infantry regiment, an artillery battalion, one each of tank, engineer, pioneer, amphibian tractor and medical companies, and one each of scout, special weapons and transport platoons. Combat Group A's infantry battalions were designated combat teams 1, 2 and 3, while Combat Group B's were called Combat Teams 4, 5 and 6. Each combat team consisted of an infantry battalion, a 75 mm pack howitzer battery, and engineer, pioneer and amphibian tractor platoons, plus small service elements. A division support group was also formed, comprising four subgroups of artillery, special weapons, engineer, pioneer, amphibian tractor, headquarters, communications, and medical elements, plus the 1st Parachute Battalion. The division was not only organised to land and fight under this structure, but also embarked its transport as groups and teams.

The use of regimental landing teams (RLTs) and battalion landing teams (BLTs) was first undertaken by the 2nd MarDiv at Tarawa (Betio) in November 1943. The first two regiments to land were organised as RLTs 2 and 8 (bearing the designation of their parent regiment), reinforced by a 105 mm artillery battalion and various combat support units. The

*A 3rd Defense Battalion twin 20 mm Mk IV anti-aircraft gun, mounted on a former 37 mm M1 gun M3A1 mount, protects the Marine beachhead on Guadalcanal. The 20 mm had a maximum range of 5,500 yards.*

BLTs were designated Red, White and Blue for 1st, 2nd and 3rd Battalions respectively, and reinforced by a 75 mm pack howitzer battalion, tank company and engineer platoon. The BLTs possessed only combat elements; all service elements supported the RLTs and the division.

Battalions and companies also task organised their assets to counter enemy capabilities more effectively. In early 1944 the 4th MarDiv organised its assault companies into 'assault and demolition teams' for the Roi-Namur landing. Companies formed six teams, each led by an officer and consisting of a four-man light machine gun group, a five-man demolitions group, a three-man bazooka group and a four-man support group (two BARs). A team was carried in an LVT(2) amtrac. The follow-on reserve companies formed 'boat teams' which were similar and were carried in an LCVP landing craft; the boat teams lacked the machine gun group.

There was no fixed organisation for Marine brigades. They were established as provisional formations to accomplish specific missions, and most of their assets would be drawn from the same division. Brigades generally consisted of one or two infantry regiments, an artillery and/or a defence battalion, and small combat support and service elements. Upon disbandment, the brigades' units would be returned to their parent division's control. Wartime brigades were designated 1st, 2nd and 3rd. A 1st Brigade was formed immediately before and during the war, and a 3rd Brigade was formed during and immediately after the war. However, despite using the same name, the later 1st and 3rd brigades carried separate lineages to the earlier ones.

# MARINE WEAPONS

Marine Corps' weapons requirements were somewhat different to those of the Army. Major restrictions were shipping space, and the fact that larger weapons could be on- and off-loaded easily on landing craft, e.g. a 105 mm howitzer's wide tyres and wheels were replaced with the narrower 2½ ton truck's so that it could be loaded in a DUKW amphibian truck. Mobility was another requirement, especially in rugged, hilly, tropical jungles. Direct fire weapons were worthless if they could not be manhandled into position to engage the enemy in confined terrain such as ravines and swamps. Vehicles were often in short supply during the early stages of amphibious landings, so many support weapons had to have manhandling capability by small crews. For example, when under attack from

*Armed with M1903 rifles fitted with M1905 bayonets, a 1st MarDiv squad searches an abandoned enemy shelter in the Solomons, 1942. (Shelby Stanton collection)*

two tanks, desperate Marines manually lifted a 37 mm AT gun over Betio's five-foot-high sea wall.

In contrast to the concern caused by massed German armour, the Japanese tank threat was minimal, and anti-tank weapons were most commonly employed to reduce enemy positions by direct fire. In the Pacific, the Marines faced a greater air threat than the Army did in Europe, so anti-aircraft weapons played a more important role. They were also employed in both direct and indirect fire roles.

Artillery played an important role in providing indirect fire support. Defence battalions initially had the principal responsibility of protecting advanced naval bases. For this they employed coast and anti-aircraft artillery. The coast defence role was soon obsolete, as the Japanese lost their ability to threaten forward bases, and the semi-mobile coast guns were subsequently replaced by towed field artillery.

Tanks were of minimal use on many of the islands the Marines fought over, due to terrain restrictions and the limited threat from enemy armour. However, a significant armour threat was encountered on islands closer to Japan, such as Saipan and Okinawa. Tanks were more often than not employed as assault weapons to defeat strong-points, and for this reason the Marines went to great lengths to develop tank-mounted flamethrowers.

The Marines were first and foremost an infantry force. The rifle was considered to be a Marine's 'best friend' and great attention was given to marksmanship. Night combat, close jungle terrain, and *banzai* attacks demanded a high density of automatic weapons. Reducing bunker and cave strong-points was of primary importance, so there was widespread use of flamethrowers, bazookas, and satchel charges.

### Infantry small arms

The Marines fielded the .30-cal. M1903 rifle in 1908, and the '03 Springfield' provided excellent service to the Corps through World War I, the 'Banana Wars', China, and into World War II. While a better made weapon, the Springfield offered no more firepower than the Japanese Arisaka; both were bolt-action with a five-round magazine. An improved version of the Springfield, the M1903A1 was standardised in 1929, but not produced until 1939, while the M1903A3 was adopted in 1942.

The most commonly used sniper rifles were the

*Wearing an Army camouflage one-piece jungle suit, a 1st MarDiv Marine uses his camouflage helmet cover to close the head opening of his OD medium weight poncho. On Cape Gloucester the incessant rain rusted equipment, rotted boots, and caused immersion foot.*

early war M1903 with a Layman No. 5A 5× telescope and the 'special reference' M1903A1s with a Unertl 8× target scope – issued in late 1943. The M1903 rifle was briefly retained after the adoption of the M1 rifle on the basis of one per squad with an M1 rifle grenade launcher fitted. It could fire both anti-tank and anti-personnel grenades.

The Marines were introduced to the Army's semi-automatic 30-cal. M1 Garand rifle on Guadalcanal in 1942, although its adoption had already been under consideration. The M1 was phased into the Corps a regiment at a time, and by 1943 the 1st, 2nd, 3rd and 4th MarDivs were armed with this rugged eight-shot rifle. Although its adoption was resisted by many 'old time' Marine marksmen (it was considered not accurate enough, and too complex for recruits), all Fleet Marine Force units were soon armed with it. The M7 rifle grenade launcher was provided for the M1 rifle.

*A 2.36 in. M1A1 bazooka team poses in the correct crew positions. The M1A1 possessed a breech protection guard not found on the M1 and an improved firing system.*

The Garand, however, was preceded by another semi-automatic, the short-lived .30-cal. M1941 rifle, the Johnson (designed by Capt. Melvin Johnson, a Marine Reservist). It offered little advantage over the M1, other than a ten-shot rotary magazine; both were the same weight, 9.5 lbs[1]. Since the M1 was far into mass production, the Johnson was dropped.

The M1 carbine was adopted in 1942 for Marines requiring a weapon more compact than a rifle but more substantial than a pistol. In fact it entirely replaced the pistol in infantry and artillery regiments between April 1943 and September 1945 when the 'pistol' was reintroduced in these units. This lightweight, 5.5 lb semi-automatic weapon had a 15-round magazine. Small numbers of folding stock M1A1 carbines were issued to parachute units in 1942, and limited use was made of the selective fire M2 carbine fielded in early 1945. The latter's 30-round 'banana clip' magazine was subsequently adopted for the M1 carbine, which was a .30-cal., but used a smaller cartridge than the M1903 and M1 rifles. Reviews on the carbine were mixed: some complained of its lack of knock-down power, while others praised its longer range and higher firepower when compared to a pistol.

The issue of sub-machine guns was relatively limited, although many units possessed more than were authorised by equipment tables. The Marines had used Thompsons since 1922 for railroad mail car guards for the postal service and during the 'Banana Wars'. The .45-cal. M1928A1 sub-machine gun saw limited use and was replaced by improved versions, the M1 and M1A1, in 1942. The heavy, 10.45 lb 'Tommy gun' was officially issued only to divisional scout and military police companies, and to raiders. The M1928A1 had used a 50-round drum or 20-round box magazine; the M1 came with a 30-round box magazine and could use the 20-round. In April 1944 it was ordered that all Thompsons be withdrawn from service and replaced by the M3A1 'grease gun' (Thompsons were to be supplied to other countries). Although the Marines retained them in small numbers, they remained ill-suited for frontline use since they sounded like Japanese 6.5 mm light machine guns.

More controversial weapons were the Reising .45-cal. M50 and M55 sub-machine guns. The Reising was adopted in 1940, with some 4,200 authorised per division. Just over 500 were assigned to an infantry regiment. Produced until 1942, by the time of Guadalcanal most had been withdrawn and relegated to Stateside guard duty. Only the parachute and raider battalions employed them to any extent. The 6.75 lb M50 had a full wood stock, while the 6.25 lb M55, intended for parachutists and tankers, had a folding wire stock and no muzzle compensator. Both used a 20-round magazine. They were plagued by jamming, a faulty magazine feed, and were prone to accidental firing.

Winchester 12-gauge M1897 and M1912 riot type shotguns were pooled at regimental level for issue as needed. These pump-action shotguns had become popular among the Marines during the 'Banana Wars'. They were not allotted in equipment tables until April 1943, when infantry regiments were authorised 100. They had a 20 in. barrel, a six-round tubular magazine, a perforated barrel hand guard and a bayonet lug. They were popular for clearing bunkers, caves, and trenches and for guarding the (rare) prisoner.

The Colt .45-cal. M1911 and M1911A1 pistols had been the standard side-arms for the Marines since 1912 (the major difference between the two was the inclusion of a grip safety on the A1, adopted in 1926). Both had a seven-round magazine. Marine aviators were issued either a Smith & Wesson Mili-

[1] All weights are for unloaded weapons.

*A 3rd Battalion, 10th Marines 75 mm M1A1 pack howitzer crew on Tulagi prepares for a fire mission protected by former Japanese position constructed of sandbags dabbed with green camouflage paint. The 16 lb. high explosive projectiles are yellow with black markings. In 1943 HE munitions were painted a camouflaging OD with yellow markings.*

tary and Police or a Colt Victory Model revolver. These were of similar design, with six-round cylinders and firing the .38-cal. special.

The .30-cal. M1918A1 and M1918A2 Browning automatic rifles provided the rifle squad's basis for firepower and tactics. The squad began the war with one BAR. Interestingly, in 1940 the Marines predicted that with the adoption of the new M1 rifle and M1919A4 machine gun, the cumbersome BAR 'should no longer be seriously considered'. The realities of combat proved otherwise, and in early 1944 squads were each authorised three BARs. The A1 (sometimes called the M1918 [Modified]), adopted in 1937, added a bipod forward of the hand guard to the original M1918. The A2 re-positioned an improved bipod near the muzzle, upgraded the rear sight, and added selective low and high rates of fire; it weighed 19.4 lbs and had a 20-round magazine.

Another squad automatic weapon was used only by parachute units. It was the Johnson .30-cal. M1941, a light machine gun similar in capability to the BAR, with a curved 20-round magazine and selective fire. It weighed only 13 lbs, but, like its rifle counterpart, was too flimsy and did not see wider use.

### Infantry crew-served weapons

The light air-cooled .30-cal. M1919A4 machine gun was issued to rifle company weapons platoons. Adopted just before the war, their numbers were gradually increased. They were also mounted on a variety of vehicles and landing craft. Weighing 31 lbs (plus a 14 lb M2 tripod), it was a comparatively heavy weapon, but extremely effective and reliable, as were all of Mr Browning's machine guns. It was fed by a 250-round web, and later a disintegrating metallic link belt. The similarly fixed M1919A5 machine gun was mounted co-axially with tank main guns.

Prior to the adoption of the M1919A4, the standard light machine gun had been the Navy .30-cal. Mk 6 Mod 1 (similar to the Army's M1917). The 27 lb bipod-mounted Lewis, with its 47-round pan magazine, was used by the 4th Marines in the Philippines, and even by the raiders, as well as aboard early war landing craft.

The standard heavy machine gun was the water-cooled .30-cal. M1917A1 machine gun. This 41 lb (with water) gun, coupled with its 53.15 lb M1917A1 tripod, proved to be an extremely effective long-range support weapon. They were initially used to arm battalion weapons companies, but the latter were eliminated in 1944, and their three heavy machine gun platoons were merged with rifle company weapons platoons.

The .50-cal. M1921A1 and M2 anti-aircraft machine guns were water-cooled weapons (their differences were internal). Filled with water, the M2 weighed 121 lbs and its pedestal mount 401 lbs. They were replaced largely by 20 mm Mk 4 guns in defence battalions. The air-cooled .50-cal. HB-M2 machine gun (HB – heavy barrel) was mounted on tanks, amtracs, and on cargo truck ring mounts for air defence. It weighed 84 lbs; its M3 tripod added 44 lbs. The '.50-cals' used 110-round metallic link belts, but a 500-round container was commonly used with the water-cooled guns.

The 60 mm M2 mortar was the standard company-level mortar and was used throughout World War II. The 81 mm M1 mortar was used at battalion level. It proved to be an effective fire support weapon and could be transported in the M6A1 hand-cart. Marines quickly found that Japanese 81 mm mortar rounds could be fired in the M1.

The Marines made little use of the portable flamethrower as an offensive weapon at first, but then small numbers were employed on Guadalcanal, and before long their use was expanded. They were especially useful in reducing bunkers and cave strong-points. The M1 flamethrower was first used,

*A fire team leader (corporal) stands ready in his fighting position bearing the tool of his trade, an M1 rifle, or 'piece'. Prior to the war the Marines used prone foxholes, they learned to dig deeper holes for better protection from artillery and to allow them to fight standing from the Japanese on Guadalcanal.*

on a limited basis, on Guadalcanal in January 1943. It suffered numerous problems and had only a 15 yd range. The M1A1 flamethrower used the new thickened fuel and had a 50 yd range; it arrived in the Pacific in July 1943. The 60 yd range M2-2 flamethrower was first used on Guam in July 1944.

## Artillery

The towed 75 mm M1897A2 gun, or 'French 75', was standard equipment for divisional direct support artillery battalions until the beginning of World War II when it was replaced by the 75 mm pack howitzer. However, two were retained per regimental weapons company. Too heavy for manhandling, the 'French 75' was replaced by the 75 mm M3 self-propelled gun in mid-1942.

*A 1st Raider Battalion light machine gun crew awaits the next Japanese attack in its water-filled position. The assistant gunner, to the left, has an M1910 pick-mattock attached to his M1941 haversack while the gunner has an M1910 entrenching tool on his.*

The compact, towed 75 mm M1A1 pack howitzer initially equipped three of the division's howitzer battalions; in mid-1944 the battalions were reduced to two. The towed 105 mm M2A1 howitzer had been introduced early in the war, with one battalion assigned to the division artillery regiment for general support. In mid-1943 an additional 105 mm battalion had been added, and in late 1945 they completely replaced the 75 mm howitzer.

Although standardised by the Army in April 1942, the 105 mm M7 self-propelled howitzer was not assigned to the Marine regimental weapons company until late 1945, when it replaced the halftrack-mounted 75 mm M3 gun. However, the actual change was made in May 1945 and the 1st and 6th Marine Divisions received the M7 in time for use on Okinawa.

The French-designed Schneider towed 155 mm M1917 howitzer was a World War I piece which saw limited use by the Marines. Its only combat use was by 4th Battalion 11th Marines on Guadalcanal. The towed 155 mm, M1 howitzer equipped some FMF artillery battalions and was assigned to one battalion of the division artillery regiment in late 1945 for general support. The cumbersome 5 in. naval guns originally used by defence battalions were soon replaced by the more mobile World War I French-designed GPF 155 mm M1918 gun. These were in turn replaced by the 155 mm M1A1 gun, which also equipped some FMF artillery battalions. This massive towed 'Long Tom' could be mounted on a fixed pedestal mount, the 'Panama mount', for coast defence.

The 4.5 in. T45 self-propelled rocket launcher equipped FMF rocket detachments, which were later assigned to divisions as platoons. It consisted of two launcher racks (14 rockets each) mounted on an

*Left: The Solomons campaign saw the first use of trained war dogs by US forces. This German Shepherd and his corporal handler patrol a beach to prevent a Japanese counterlanding.*

*Right: Col. Lewis 'Chesty' B. Puller, Commander, 7th Marines, directs a subordinate at Cape Gloucester, Western New Britain, providing a good view of the M1941 suspenders.*

International 1 ton 4×4 truck. In 1944 the barrage rockets were also mounted aboard landing craft, Infantry (Rocket)-LCI(R).

Various marks of modified obsolete 3, 5, 6 and 7 in. naval guns were employed for coastal defence by the defence battalions. These semi-mobile pieces were fitted on awkward concrete and timber mounts that required a great deal of time and effort to emplace. The 5 in. 51-cal. gun was the most common (removed from battleships undergoing modernisation), but was replaced by towed 155 mm pieces in 1942–43.

### Anti-aircraft artillery

The 60-round magazine-fed, fully-automatic Oerlikon 20 mm Mk 4 anti-aircraft and anti-tank gun (the same as those mounted aboard ships) was more effective against aircraft than tanks. However, its high profile, weight and bulk limited its usefulness as an anti-bunker weapon in rugged terrain, and it was replaced by the 37 mm M3 anti-tank gun in 1942 in regimental AT platoons.

The towed 10-round clip-fed Colt 37 mm M1 anti-aircraft gun was used by some defence battalions as a light anti-aircraft gun, but was largely replaced by the more effective 40 mm. Some defence battalions removed the 37 mm gun from its mount and replaced it with twin 20 mm Mk 4 guns to provide a more mobile weapon than the 20 mm's stationary mount.

The four-round clip-fed Bofors 40 mm M1 anti-aircraft gun was one of the most widely employed anti-aircraft weapons in World War II, used by virtually all combatants. It was, however, poorly suited as an anti-tank weapon due to its size. A towed automatic weapon, it was used by divisional special weapons battalions until mid-1944 and by defence and, later, anti-aircraft artillery battalions.

The 3 in. M3 anti-aircraft gun initially equipped defence battalions, but was later relegated to training purposes; its large towed mount and short range limited its usefulness, and it was replaced by the 90 mm M1 anti-aircraft gun. Standardised in early 1941, it equipped divisional special weapons battalions until mid-1943, and was widely used by the defence and, later, anti-aircraft artillery battalions.

### Anti-tank weapons

Standardised in February 1942, the 37 mm M6 self-propelled anti-tank gun equipped special weapons battalions until it was phased out in mid-1943. It consisted of an M3 AT gun mounted on a ¾ ton 4×4 truck. While mobile enough, it was difficult to manoeuvre into firing position, in close terrain, especially since it often had to be backed into position, as forward firing required its barrel to be raised too high.

The lightweight 37 mm M3A1 anti-tank gun was copied from the standard German AT gun. It replaced the 20 mm gun in 1942, and equipped both special weapons battalions and regimental weapons companies. While the Army found it to be of limited use as an AT weapon, due to the heavier German armour it faced, it was quite capable of dealing with most Japanese tanks. Its main use was as an anti-bunker weapon, and it could be manhandled through difficult terrain (although there were complaints of its limited effectiveness in this role).

The 75 mm M3 self-propelled anti-tank gun had a forward firing M1897A4 gun mounted on an M3 halftrack. Standardised in November 1941, it equipped both special weapons battalions and regimental weapons companies; it was concentrated in the weapons companies in mid-1944, but began to be replaced by the 105 mm self-propelled in 1944. In North Africa the Army had found the 75 mm to be a poor tank destroyer, but the Marines employed it principally as an assault gun for knocking out fortified positions and for indirect artillery fire. It was commonly known as the SPM (Self-Propelled Mount).

The 2.36 in. M1 rocket launcher, or 'bazooka', was adopted in 1942 on a limited scale, mainly as an AT weapon. Its numbers within the division was almost doubled in mid-1943 when it was found to be highly effective against bunkers. Besides being used to equip infantry units, it was issued to other units for AT protection; but there were no dedicated crews. The slightly improved M1A1 replaced the M1 in mid-1944, but their numbers were reduced in support units due to the limited threat posed by Japanese armour. In 1944 the M1A1 began to be replaced by the 2.36 in. M9A1 and M18 rocket launchers. These improved bazookas had a longer range due to a lengthened tube which could be broken down into two sections for carrying. The two new launchers were identical, except the M18 was developed for use in the Pacific theatre so was made of aluminium to prevent rusting.

The massive Boys .55-cal. Mk I anti-tank rifle was used by raider battalions. The 36 lb weapon was mainly employed to knock-out bunkers. It was bolt-action fed by a five-round magazine and fitted with a bipod.

## Tanks

The M2A4 light tank, introduced in 1939, was little used by the Marines; the M3 tank was the principal model employed. The M2 mounted a 37 mm M5 gun and up to five .30-cal. M1919A4 and A5 machine guns (side sponsons, bow, turret top, main gun co-axial). The General Stuart M3 and M3A1 light tanks were introduced in early 1941. The M3A3 light tank came out in late 1942. Differences between the models were mainly internal. All mounted either a 37 mm M5 or M6 gun and three M1919A4 and A5 machine guns (five on the M3; the others lacked sponson guns). They began to be replaced by the M4-series in mid-1944. The Marines retro-fitted the Satan A-H1B flamethrower to M3A1 tanks atop their turrets. A small number of the M5A1 light tank, an upgraded variant of the M3-series, were employed in early 1944. Its armament was the same as the M3A3's.

The General Sherman M4A2 and M4A3 medium tanks mounted a 75 mm M3 gun, two M1919A4 and A5 machine guns (bow and co-axial), and a .50-cal. HB-M2 atop the turret. Some M4A3s were armed with a 105 mm M4 howitzer and employed as assault tanks. The M4A2 was actually preferred, as its diesel engine used the same fuel as landing craft, thus easing logistics requirements; the M4A3 was petrol powered. Some M4s were fitted with an E4-5 flamethrower in lieu of the 75 mm main gun. The M3-4-3 was a flamethrower kit retro-fitted to some M4s in place of the bow machine gun.

## Other combat vehicles

The White 4×4 M3A1 scout car was used by the 1st and 2nd MarDivs' scout companies from 1941 to early 1942. These open-topped 'armoured trucks' mounted HB-M2 and M1917A1 machine guns.

*An 11th Marines 75 mm pack howitzer, in full recoil, crew at Cape Gloucester cuts charges on the next round. Both wear Army camouflage one-piece jungle suits*

Sometimes additional M1919A4 machine guns were mounted. The scout cars were ill-suited for reconnaissance on tropical islands, and were replaced by machine gun-armed ¼-ton jeeps.

The Landing Vehicle, Tracked Mk 1, or LVT1 amphibian tractor ('amtrac'), was produced between 1941 and 1943 as an improved means of landing troops and cargo on hostile beaches. Also known as the 'Alligator', these early amtracs usually mounted HB-M2 and M1917A1 machine guns. (However, many variations of machine gun mountings were used on this and on later LVTs.) The Alligator was unarmoured, had no rear ramp, and carried 20 troops or 4,500 lbs of cargo. It was first used in the Gilberts, but remained in use throughout the war. All cargo LVTs had a three-man crew.

The improved LVT2 and LVT(A)2 amphibian tractors, or 'Water Buffalos', were unarmoured and armoured respectively. They usually mounted an HB-M2 and three M1919A4 machine guns. They still lacked a rear ramp. They were in production from early 1942 to 1944, and were first used in the Marshalls. As with all later models, they carried 24 troops or 6,500 lbs of cargo (LVT3 carried 8,000 lbs).

The unarmoured LVT3 amphibian tractor, or 'Brushmaster', was built between 1943 and 1945, but the only action it saw was on Okinawa in 1945. It was the first version with a ramp, allowing the transport of a 37 mm AT gun and jeep, a 75 mm pack howitzer or a 105 mm howitzer. It mounted HB-M2 and M1919A4 machine guns.

Similar to the LVT2, the late war LVT4 amphibian tractor was unarmoured, but had a rear ramp and could carry the same cargo as the LVT3. It usually mounted HB-M2 and M1919A4 machine guns. They were built between 1943 and 1945 and saw earlier service than the LVT3 (due to production delays with the latter), at Saipan in 1944.

The LVT(A)1 amphibian tank, or 'amtank', was based on the LVT1 chassis, but was armoured and fitted with an M3A1 tank turret with a 37 mm M6 gun and co-axial M1919A5 machine gun. Two M1919A4 machine guns were mounted at man-holes behind the turret, allowing fire to the flanks and rear.

*The face of combat fatigue, a 1st MarDiv machine gunner carries a .30 cal. M1917A1 heavy machine gun as his unit is relieved from the line, Cape Gloucester. Near the pistol grip is the gun's traversing and elevating mechanism, which would be linked to the tripod.*

It had a six-man crew. Some were fitted with flamethrowers.

The LVT(A)4 amphibian tank was based on the LVT4 chassis, but was armoured and fitted with an open-topped turret from the M8 self-propelled howitzer with a 75 mm M3 howitzer and turret-top HB-M2 machine gun. It had a five-man crew.

All marks of LVTs were modified for special support purposes and included command, recovery, and engineer versions. Heavy fire support weapons, ranging from flamethrowers to 20 mm and 40 mm automatic guns and 4.5 in. rocket launchers, were fitted as required.

A small number of radio-equipped M3 personnel carriers were added to the division in late 1945 as command halftracks. They usually mounted an M1919A4 machine gun.

*Members of the 1st MarDiv Scout Company patrol the Natamo River, Cape Gloucester, aboard a 16 ft. LCR(L). The rubber boat was designed to carry 10 men.*

*A 90 mm M1 anti-aircraft gun of the 3rd Defense Battalion defends the Bougainville beachhead. The spotter, standing atop the sandbag parapet, wears a Mk 2 'talker' helmet.*

Although the 2½ ton DUKW-353 amphibian truck was standardised by the Army in late 1942, the Marines did not begin using the 'Duck'[1] until 1944, at Eniwetok. It had a 6×6 chassis, was fully amphibious, and could transport 25 Marines or 5,000 lbs of cargo. One in four were fitted with an HB-M2 machine gun ring mount.

# MARINE UNITS

The Marine Corps grew rapidly with America's involvement in World War II. From two under-strength divisions, two small aircraft groups and a smattering of support units in December 1941, it swelled to an army-level command of two corps, six divisions, five aircraft wings, scores of support units and a large Stateside supporting establishment by VJ-Day.

## Unit designation practices

The numbering of Marine units was quite straightforward. The six divisions were numbered in sequence of activation. Marine regiments were designated in blocks by functional type: 1st–9th and 21st–29th were infantry, 10th–15th artillery, and 16th–20th engineer. Regimental titles did not include a functional designation; the initiated would know, for example, that the 10th Marines was artillery. For convenience, in this book artillery and engineer regiments will be identified as such in parentheses; it is emphasised that this is not part of their designation. Since 1930 it was not required for 'regiment' to be included in a unit's designation, e.g. 4th Marines. The 1st Parachute Regiment, 1st and 2nd Raider Regiments, 7th and 8th Service Regiments were not numbered in the above series, and their functional designations, as well as 'Regiment', were included in their titles.

With the exception of regiments, which were assigned to divisions almost at random, all other units within a division carried the division's designation, e.g. 1st Signal Battalion. FMF units were numbered in sequence by functional category. Caution must be taken not to assume that every unit designated, e.g. '1st', was assigned to the 1st MarDiv. Amphibious corps troops units carried the designation of their parent corps, e.g. III or V Corps Signal Battalion; I Corps units were designated '1st Corps . . .'.

Battalions were designated 1st–3rd in infantry and engineer regiments. Artillery regiments had four or five battalions. Companies were designated in alphabetic sequence through the regiment, e.g. Companies A, B, C, D were assigned to 1st Battalion and so on up through Company M, with four companies per battalion; Companies D, H and M were weapons. When weapons companies were dissolved in 1944, the rifle companies were not re-lettered (the sole exception was the 29th Marines, formed at the time of the reorganisation). Five-battalion artillery regiments possessed up to Battery S, with three lettered firing batteries per battalion. Traditionally, there was no company or battery 'J'. Regimental weapons companies were designated simply, e.g. Weapons Company, 3rd Marines.

Provisional Marine brigades were numbered in sequence of activation. Early in the war, there were three such brigades on active duty. Once these brigades had been disbanded, the next new provisional brigade to be formed would be designated '1st' and the series would start again.

## Fleet Marine Force

The FMF traces its origins from 1913, when the Marine Advanced Base Force was formed. It consisted of a two-regiment brigade intended to seize

---

[1] Its nickname was derived from its General Motors model designation: 'D' – year model (1942), 'U' – amphibian, 'K' – all-wheel drive, and 'W' – duel rear axles.

20

*Bougainville, 1944. The sign reads, 'SNiPER iNN - COVER CHARGE 1 JAP'. A sandbagged fighting position doubles as living quarters with the addition of a camouflage shelter half.*

and/or defend overseas naval bases in support of expeditionary operations. It was redesignated the East Coast Expeditionary Force in 1922, and a similar force was soon established on the West Coast. These two forces were redesignated the East and West Coast Fleet Marine Forces in 1933. The 1st and 2nd Marine Brigades, later expanded to divisions, were components of these forces. Two corps-size amphbibious forces were activated in June and March 1941. Both corps endured a bewildering series of designations before they received their final titles of Amphibious Corps, Atlantic Fleet and Pacific Fleet in March and April 1942, respectively. These were not tactical formations, but provided joint amphibious training to Marine and Army divisions.

When V Amphibious Corps was formed in September 1943 and deployed to the central Pacific to join I Marine Amphibious Corps, it was decided that a higher level controlling headquarters was needed. Administrative and service units of both corps were reassigned to V Amphibious Corps Administrative Command on 10 April 1944. On 11 June this organisation was reformed as Administrative Command, Fleet Marine Force, Pacific. On 24 August Provisional Headquarters, Fleet Marine Force, Pacific was established. Both the Provisional Headquarters and the Administrative Command were consolidated on 17 September 1944 to form Fleet Marine Force, Pacific (FMFPac) under the command of Lt.Gen. Holland M. 'Howlin' Mad' Smith. FMFPac and its predecessors were headquartered at Pearl Harbor, where it remained. FMFPac had operational command of the I (later, III) and V Amphibious Corps; the six divisions; 1st 2nd, 3rd and 4th Marine Aircraft Wings, and attached Army divisions and Allied units.

## Amphibious corps

Like the evolution of the FMF, the development of amphibious corps was complex. In 1941–42 the Amphibious Corps, Atlantic Fleet and the PhibCorps, Pacific Fleet were organised to provide amphibious training. **I Marine Amphibious Corps** (IMAC) was established on 1 October 1942 and deployed to the south Pacific in the same month under the command of Maj.Gen. Alexander 'Sunny Jim' Vandegrift. It controlled Marine operations on Guadalcanal in 1942 and oversaw the reduction of the remainder of the Solomon Islands until early 1944. In September 1943 Maj.Gen. Charles Barrett assumed command, but died three weeks later. Vandegrift briefly reassumed command, and Maj.Gen. Roy S. Geiger took over in November. IMAC moved to the Bismarck Archipelago in March 1944 to seize islands in that area. The 1st, 2nd and 3rd (briefly) MarDivs habitually served under IMAC. On 15 April 1944 IMAC's support units were transferred to the V Amphibious Corps Administrative Command, and the tactical units were redesignated III Amphibious Corps.

*A 10th Marines, 2nd MarDiv, 75 mm pack howitzer crew undergoes training, Hawke Bay, New Zealand, in preparation for the Tarawa assault. Note the gun pointer's reversed helmet to allow him unhindered use of the sight.*

*Tarawa bound Marines of the 2nd MarDiv descend a debarkation net into their landing craft. They wear camouflage utility uniforms, M26 life belts, gas mask cases, and M1 carbines indicating a support unit. Gloves were often worn when descending nets to prevent injuries. Only the vertical ropes were gripped to prevent a Marine above from stepping on one's hands.*

**III Amphibious Corps** (IIIAC) was given the mission of seizing Guam in July and August 1944, and it went on to take Peleliu in September and October. The Army's 77th Infantry Division was attached to IIIAC for these operations. IIIAC then moved to Guadalcanal to prepare for the Okinawa assault subordinate to Tenth Army. The operation began in April 1945 and lasted until July, after which it moved to the Marians. The 1st, 3rd and 6th MarDivs (and 1st Marine Brigade prior to 6th MarDiv's formation) habitually served under IIIAC. The corps was deployed to North China in September 1945 to disarm Japanese forces. It was redesignated Marine Forces, China on 10 June 1946, and was greatly down-sized.

**Amphibious Corps, Pacific Fleet** (PhibCorpsPacFlt), formed in April 1942, played an important role controlling Marine and Army tactical units not assigned to the operational IMAC. Under the command of Maj.Gen. Holland Smith, it was based at Pearl Harbor. Its assets were later redesignated V Amphibious Corps.

**V Amphibious Corps** (VAC) was formed on 25 August 1943 at Pearl Harbor from PhibCorpsPacFlt. It originally included VAC Administrative Command, but this was redesignated Administrative Command, FMFPac on 10 April 1944 (which in turn was redesignated FMFPac in June). Formed as the amphibious landing force for Fifth Fleet to support central Pacific operations, VAC was commanded by Maj.Gen. Holland Smith. Its first mission was to seize the Gilbert Islands in preparation for future efforts in the Marshalls. This included the controversial assault on Tarawa and the attached Army's 27th Infantry Division's seizure of Makin; both operations took place in November 1943. In January and February 1944 the VAC, along with the attached 7th and 27th Infantry Divisions, seized Roi-Namur, Kwajalin and Eniwetok in the Marshalls. Its next task was to secure the Marianas. This it did from June to August 1944, which included seizing Saipan, Tinian, and Guam in concert with the Army's XXIV Corps. Maj.Gen. Harry Schmidt took command of VAC in July. VAC's next mission took place in February 1945, when it assaulted Iwo Jima. The island was secured a month later, but VAC's losses were such that it was months before its three divisions were again ready for combat. VAC landed in Japan at Yokosuka and Kyushu in September 1945, where it remained as an occupation force until January 1946; it was deactivated the following month. The 2nd, 4th and 5th MarDivs were habitually assigned to VAC, while the 3rd was briefly attached.

Various service units were assigned to amphibious corps troops. For the most part these consisted of: corps headquarters and service battalion; corps

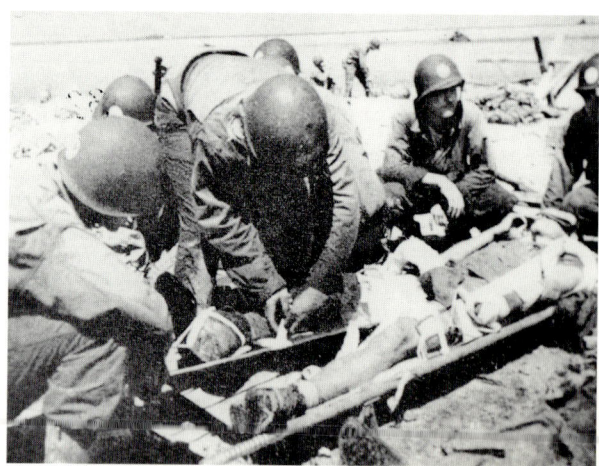

*Navy corpsmen splint a Marine's shattered leg at a beach aid station, Tawara, prior to his evacuation by returning landing craft. The painted white discs used to identify corpsmen can be seen on their helmets.*

signal battalion; corps motor transport battalion; corps medical battalion; corps artillery (not in IMAC); and corps evacuation hospital. IMAC also possessed the 1st Corps Naval Construction and 1st Corps Tank Battalions.

### Marine divisions

The formation of the first permanent Marine brigade was on September 1935, when the 1st Marine Brigade was raised at Quantico, Virginia. It was built around the 5th Marines and the 1st Battalion, 10th Marines (artillery). This was followed by the 2nd Marine Brigade, formed on 1 July 1936 at San Diego, California. It deployed to China from 1937–38. Initially it included only the 6th Marines, but the 8th Marines was raised and assigned to the Brigade in April 1940 and the 2nd Battalion, 10th Marines (artillery) was added in December. These two brigades provided the core for the 1st and 2nd MarDivs when they were activated in February 1941. The two new divisions were at less than 60 per cent strength and possessed only minimal combat support and service units by the time of Pearl Harbor.

The **1st Marine Division** ('The Old Breed') was activated at Guantánamo Bay, Cuba, on 1 February 1941 from the 1st Marine Brigade. It soon relocated to New River, North Carolina (renamed Camp Lejeune in 1944), and trained for overseas deployment. It consisted of the 1st, 5th, 7th, 11th (artillery) and 17th (engineer) Marines. The division formed the 3rd Marine Brigade in March 1942 and deployed it to Samoa as a defence force. The division deployed to New Zealand in May. It landed on Guadalcanal on 7 August 1942 (7th Marines did not arrive from Samoa until 18 September), and fought until late December, when it was withdrawn to Australia for a year-long rest and refit. It landed on Western New Britain on 26 December 1943 under Sixth Army. There followed a number of amphibious operations on other Bismarck Archipelago islands and along the New Britain coast. These operations were completed in April 1944 and the division was then moved to Pavuvu in the Russells for rest. On 15 September 1944 the division, under IIIAC, assaulted Peleliu in the Palaus Islands, the western-most group in the Carolines, and encountered the war's first deadly cave defences. It was relieved on 16 October, and moved back to Pavuvu, then on 1 April 1945 as-

*A 10th Marines 75 mm pack howitzer crew fires point blank at a Japanese strong point, Tarawa, 1943. They wear a mixture of sage green and camouflage utilities.*

saulted Okinawa, where it fought until 21 June. It was deployed to North China on 30 September 1945 as an occupation force and to disarm Japanese forces in Hopeh Province, then was moved to Camp Pendleton in June 1947. (It has remained there to this day, and has participated in every major post-World War II US conflict.)

The **2nd Marine Division** was activated on 1 February 1941 from the 2nd Marine Brigade at San Diego, California, where it trained for overseas deployment. It provided assets for the 1st Marine Brigade, sent to reinforce Iceland's defences, and for the 3rd Marine Brigade to defend Samoa. Elements were deployed to the Pacific in mid-1942 and attached to the 1st MarDiv. They included the 2nd Marines; 3rd Battalion, 10th Marines (artillery); and 2nd Special Weapons Battalion. They landed on islands near Guadalcanal on 7 August to support operations on the larger island. The 8th Marines and 1st Battalion, 10th Marines further reinforced the 1st MarDiv in early November. On 4 January 1943 Advance Echelon, Headquarters, 2nd MarDiv arrived with the 6th Marines and 2nd Battalion, 10th Marines, and assumed command of the divisional elements that had arrived earlier. The Advance Echelon continued operations until 8 February, but most divisional supporting units did not participate. During the conclusion of the Guadalcanal campaign, a

*Numar, 1944, Marines await pause in their push across the island in under two days. This BAR man holds an M1918A1 BAR (magazine detached) with the flash hider removed to reduce its length.*

provisional joint force was formed by the Army's XIV Corps on 25 January 1943 from elements of the 2nd MarDiv and the Army's Americal Division. The 2nd MarDiv's Advanced Echelon Headquarters acted as the Composite Army-Marine Division's Headquarters; other elements of both divisions were exhausted from prolonged combat[1]. The CAM Division was dissolved on 9 February and its units returned to their respective divisions' control. The 2nd MarDiv reassembled in New Zealand in early 1943 for rest and retraining. It assaulted Betio Island (Tarawa) on 20 November 1943 and suffered appalling losses. It was then moved to Hawaii for recovery and rebuilding. The division assaulted Saipan on 15 June 1944 and then neighbouring Tinian on 26 July. It conducted mop-up operations on Saipan and Tinian through to the end of 1944. On 1 April 1945 the Division assaulted Okinawa and returned to Saipan on 15 June. It landed at Sasebo on Kyushu (the southern-most island of Japan) on 16 September 1945 for occupation duty, and remained there until July 1946 when it moved to Camp Lejeune, North Carolina (where it has remained ever since).

The **3rd Marine Division** was activated on 16 September 1942 with the Advance Echelon (9th Marines) at Camp Elliott, California, and Rear Echelon (19th (engineer), 21st and 23rd Marines) at New River, North Carolina. The 12th Marines (artillery) was not activated until February 1943. In early 1943 the division moved to New Zealand, where the newly formed 3rd Marines joined it in June, in place of the 23rd Marines, which had remained in the US. The division moved to Guadalcanal for additional training and then took part in the remainder of the Solomon Islands campaign under IMAC, by assaulting Bougainville on 1 November 1943. The division returned to Guadalcanal on 16 January 1944. It was to have assaulted New Ireland in April 1944, but the operation was cancelled. In June 1944 the division moved to the Marianas and assaulted Guam on 21 July under IIIAC. The operation was completed on 10 August, but the division remained there until February 1945. It landed on Iwo Jima on 24 February as VAC reinforcements; the division's 3rd Marines remained afloat as the VAC reserve. The division fought on Iwo until the operation's end on 16 March 1945. In April it was returned to Guam to prepare for the invasion of Japan, but was deactivated on 18 December 1945. (It was reactivated in 1952, and has remained active.)

The **4th Marine Division** was activated on 16 August 1943 at Camp Pendleton, California, from units in training: 14th (artillery), 20th (engineer), 23rd, 24th and 25th Marines. It departed for the Pacific in January 1944 and on 1 February assaulted the twin islands of Roi-Namur (part of the Kwajalein-Majuro Occupation in the Marshalls) under VAC. The division relocated to Hawaii for rest and then assaulted Saipan on 15 June 1944 under VAC's Northern Troops and Landing Forces. On 24 July the division assaulted Tinian and fought until 1 August. It was soon moved to Hawaii for rest. On 19 February 1945 it assaulted Iwo Jima, and fought there until 16 March, again returning to Hawaii to prepare for the invasion of Japan. Instead, it moved to Camp Pendleton, California, and was deactivated on 28 November 1945. (It was reactivated as a reserve division in 1962, and has remained as such ever since.)

The **5th Marine Division** ('The Spearhead') was activated on 21 January 1944 at Camp Pendleton with the 26th, 27th and 28th Marines. The deactivated parachute battalions provided the cadre for the 28th Marines. It also included the 13th (artillery) and

---

[1] CAM Division's Marine components were 6th Marines, and 1st, 2nd and 3rd Battalions, 10th Marines (artillery). Army components were 147th (2nd Battalion) and 182nd (3rd Battalion) Infantry Regiments, and the Americal Division Artillery with 221st (155 mm), 245th, 246th and 247th (105 mm) Field Artillery Battalions. The Americal Division was formed on New Caledonia from a mix of separate Army units and its designation derived from the contraction of 'AMERIcans on New CALedonia'.

*Members of the 4th MarDiv Headquarters drag a Japanese prisoner from a Numar pillbox. White stencilled unit markings can be seen on two of the men's backs.*

16th (engineer – deactivated prior to overseas deployment) Marines. The division moved in phases to Hawaii later in the year and was completely assembled by October. It assaulted Iwo Jima, its only combat operation, on 19 February 1945 as part of VAC, and fought there until the end on 27 March. It moved to Hawaii for rest and then landed at Nagasaki, on Kyushu Island, Japan, on 22 September 1945 for occupation duty. It was withdrawn on 15 December, moved to Camp Pendleton, and deactivated in January 1946. (It was reactivated at Camp Pendleton in 1966 to replace the 1st MarDiv that had deployed to Vietnam, and was deactivated in 1970 upon the 1st MarDiv's return.)

The 1st Provisional Marine Brigade was formed from separate units in mid-1944 for the Guam operation (see below). The **6th Marine Division** was activated on 7 September 1944 on Guadalcanal, using the 1st Provisional Marine Brigade as a core (4th and 22nd Marines). Other personnel were provided by anti-aircraft and deactivated defence battalions, along with units from the US – 15th (artillery) and 29th Marines. The division was assembled on Guam and assigned to IIIAC. It assaulted Okinawa, its only combat operation, on 1 April 1945, and fought there until 21 June. It returned to Guam, and the 4th Marines accompanied the Fleet Landing Force for the occupation of Japan, being the first Marine unit to land. The division was deployed to North China as an occupation force, arriving on 11 October. It operated in Shantung Province until deactivated in Tsingtao, China, on 31 March 1946. Its remaining units were formed into the 3rd Marine Brigade. (The division has not since been reactivated.)

### Provisional Marine brigades

The five provisional Marine brigades formed just prior to, during and immediately after the war were tied directly to specific divisions. Their assets were provided by their parent division, and they were returned to them upon the brigades' deactivation. There is one exception: the 1st Marine Brigade formed for the Guam campaign was comprised of separate units and became the core of a new division.

The **1st Marine Brigade (Provisional)** was formed on 16 June 1941 at Charleston, South Carolina, with units drawn from the 2nd MarDiv. Given the task of reinforcing British defences on Iceland, to allow the garrison to be reduced for more judicious use elsewhere, the brigade departed on 22 June and arrived in Iceland on 7 July (notably, prior to America's entry into the war). It established defensive positions along the coast, mainly north of Reykjavik. On 22 September the brigade was placed under the command of the US Army's Iceland Base Command. It was relieved by Army units and returned to the US between February and March 1942. It was disbanded on 25 March in New York City, and its units rejoined the 2nd MarDiv in California.

The **2nd Marine Brigade** was formed by 2nd

*An M5A1 light tank, 'Hothead', of the 4th Tank Battalion supports the advance of 4th MarDiv troops on Numar. White bands have been hand painted over its forest green base colour.*

MarDiv on 14 December 1941 at Camp Elliott, California. It arrived with the 8th Marines in American Samoa on 19 January 1942. The first elements of Marine Aircraft Group 13 arrived in April, and the brigade was later joined by the 7th and 8th Defense Battalions. The 3rd Marines replaced the 8th on 14 September 1942. It was dissolved in January 1943, and its assets returned to 2nd MarDiv control.

The **3rd Marine Brigade** was formed by 1st MarDiv on 21 March 1942 at New River, North Carolina, and deployed to British Samoa on 19 January 1942. The Brigade's 7th Marines redeployed to Guadalcanal, arriving on 16 September, and rejoined the 1st MarDiv. The 3rd Brigade remained on Western Samoa's Upolu and Savai'i Islands until late 1943, under the Samoa Defense Force, along with the separate 22nd Marines (Reinforced); 147th Infantry Regiment (Army)2nd, 5th, 7th and 8th Defense Battalions, and 4th Marine Base Defense Aircraft Wing, garrisoning Samoa area islands.

A new **1st Provisional Marine Brigade** was formed on Guadalcanal from the separate 4th and 22nd Marines (Reinforced) in mid-1944. The only Marine brigade of the era to see combat, it landed on Guam on 21 July 1944 and fought there until 15 August. It was moved back to Guadalcanal and provided the core of the new 6th MarDiv in September. The Brigade's 22nd Marines was formed as a separate regiment in 1942, garrisoned Samoa through 1943, and participated in the Kwajalein and Eniwetok occupations in early 1944 as the brigade-size Tactical Group 1, VAC. The 4th Marines was formed from the disbanded raider battalions in 1944, and participated in the Enirau landing in March 1944.

A new **3rd Marine Brigade** was formed, around the 4th Marines, on 1 April 1946 in Tsingtao, China, when the 6th MarDiv was deactivated. (A 3rd Marine Brigade had served in Shanghai from 1927 to 1929 and the new brigade carried its number.) The Brigade was deactivated on 10 June 1946 and provided the core of Marine Forces, Tsingtao, itself disbanded in September 1947.

## Fleet Marine Force, Pacific units

A variety of mostly battalion-size combat support and service units were assigned to FMFPac. These in turn were assigned to amphibious corps and divisions

*Beachheads quickly became crowded and cluttered after the initial landing with a continuous flow of reinforcements, service troops, and supplies competing for space. A Landing Vehicle, Tracked (Armored) Mk1 (LVT(A)1) 'amtank' is forced to wait at the water's edge. In the background a 114 ft. Landing Craft, Tank Mk V (LCT(5)) dwarfs an LCVP.*

to support specific operations. They could then revert to FMFPac control or be reassigned to other corps or divisions. Multiple-battalion provisional artillery, anti-aircraft artillery and LVT (amphibian tractor) groups were formed to support major landing operations. Army units often augmented these.

The 22-man Observer Group was formed in January 1942 as an experimental unit from 5th Marines personnel. Originally part of a joint force preparing for the invasion of North Africa, it was transferred to the PhibCorpsPacFlt in September. The Observer Group was expanded to form the Amphibious Reconnaissance Company, PhibCorpsPacFlt on 7 January 1943 at Camp Pendleton, with 98 troops. It was redesignated Amphibious Reconnaissance Company, VAC on 25 August, and relocated to Hawaii in October. It was expanded to the 303-man, two-company Amphibious Reconnaissance Battalion, VAC on 14 April 1944, and was again redesignated Amphibious Reconnaissance Battalion, FMFPac[1] on 26 August on Hawaii. This unit operated mostly in support of VAC. It was deactivated on 24 September 1945. IMAC provided personnel to the combined Special Services Unit No. 1 in April 1943. It was also comprised of Army personnel, Australian soldiers and New Britain and New Guinea natives. It served under Sixth Army until disbanded at the war's end.

[1] See Osprey Elite 55, *Marine Recon 1940–1990*.

*Navy corpsmen treat 4th MarDiv troops on Roi-Numar prior to evacuation. Plasma bottles are suspended from a makeshift support, a rope tied between two bamboo poles.*

The concept of Marine parachute battalions[1] emerged in May 1940, and training of the first parachutists began in October at Lakehurst, New Jersey, under Navy tutelage. The first unit formed was 1st Platoon, Company A, 2nd Parachute Battalion at San Diego in February 1941. This unit provided the core of the first full unit – the 1st Parachute Battalion formed at Quantico on 15 August 1941. It was to fight on Guadalcanal alongside the raiders. Company B, 2nd Parachute Battalion was activated on 23 July 1941 and the full battalion on 1 October. The 3rd Battalion was activated on 16 September 1942 at San Diego. It was originally planned that the battalions would be organic to divisions as reconnaissance and raiding forces, but this never fully germinated. They were actually assigned, but operated under higher command control most of the time. The 1st Parachute Regiment was activated at Tontouta, New Caledonia, on 1 April 1943 to control all three battalions in the Bougainville and New Georgia operations. The two parachute schools, located at San Diego and New River, were activated in February and May 1942 respectively; they also trained personnel for the air delivery sections organic to corps headquarters and service battalions. The 4th Parachute Battalion was formed from the cadre and students of the New River Parachute School, on 1 July 1943, but was never deployed overseas. The parachute units made no combat jumps, although jumps were planned on Kolombangra and Kavieng. On 30 December 1943 all units were ordered to deactivate. The 1st Parachute Regiment was deactivated on 29 February 1944 at San Diego, and used as a cadre for the 28th Marines.

The idea of raider battalions developed in early 1941, when Marine officers visited the British Commandos. The Marine Corps soon split into two schools of thought. Many opposed the organisation of specialised raider units, maintaining that all Marine units were capable of raider operations by nature of their training. (The Marines still maintain this policy, and continue to resist the formation of 'an elite within an elite'.) Nevertheless, the 1st and 2nd Separate Battalions were formed as raider units by the 1st and 2nd MarDivs on 6 January and 4 February 1942 respectively. They were redesignated the 1st (Quantico) and 2nd (San Diego) Raider Battalions on 16 and 19 February, respectively. The 3rd Raider Battalion was formed on Samoa from 3rd Marine Brigade volunteers on 20 September 1942. It was followed by the 4th Raider Battalion at Linda Vista, California, on 23 October. In August it was directed that provisional raider battalions be formed in the 2nd, 7th and 8th Marines. This order was countermanded, but not before a 2nd Provisional Raider Battalion had been raised on Espíritu Santo, only to be disbanded when the 'real' 2nd Battalion arrived.

The 1st Raider Regiment was activated on 15 March 1943 to control the 1st and 4th Battalions during the New Georgia operation. The 2nd Raider Regiment (Provisional) was formed on 12 September to control the 2nd and 3rd Battalions during the Bougainville operation. The Raider Training Battalion provided replacements from Camp Pendleton from February 1943 to January 1944. In December 1943 it was directed that the raiders be reorganised as conventional infantry and the planned 5th and 6th Raider Battalions were deleted from the Force Operating Plan. The 4th Marines were reformed almost entirely from raiders at Tassafarougu, Guadalcanal, on 1 February 1944. It had been planned to reactivate the 4th Marines, lost at Corregidor in 1942, using particularly distinguished units.

Defence battalions were first organised in 1939 to defend advanced naval bases, namely island bases in

---

[1] These units were often referred to as 'Paramarines', a term the Marines frown upon as it implies they were 'half-marines'.

*A 2nd MarDiv 75 mm M3 anti-tank gun halftrack fires on an enemy strong point on Saipan, 1944. The crew's gear is slung on the outside hull. Common Marine vehicle base colours were forest green shade 23 and the darker OD shade 9.*

the Pacific and Caribbean. By early 1944 the 1st–18th and 51st and 52nd Defense Battalions had been formed. As the US assumed the offensive, the battalions were employed to protect beachheads from enemy air attack and from amphibious landings in the rear areas. The artillery soon began firing support for ground forces. The changing nature of the war and Japan's inability to mount serious counter-offensives led to most of the defence battalions being converted to anti-aircraft artillery by mid-1944, and their artillery group's assets provided the core for FMF artillery battalions. Only the 6th on Midway and the coloured 51st and 52nd Defense Battalions remained.

The 1st–18th Anti-aircraft Artillery Battalions (no 6th) were formed between April and September 1944, by converting defence battalions. The battalions were assigned to FMF artillery and placed in support of corps, in general support of divisions, or employed to defend forward naval operating bases on various Pacific islands. Only the 2nd, 5th, 7th 8th, 12th and 16th were committed to major combat operations. All but the 1st were deactivated after the war.

The 1st–6th 155 mm Howitzer Artillery Battalions and 7th–12th 155 mm Gun Artillery Battalions were formed during 1944. They were assigned to corps artillery and placed in general support of divisions. Only the 10th and 12th did not see combat. All were deactivated after the war.

The 1st–11th Amphibian Tractor Battalions proved to be among the most valuable of units employed in the Pacific. All but the 7th and 8th were committed to combat. The 1st–5th Battalions had originally been assigned to the 1st–5th MarDivs, but were transferred to FMF troops in May 1944. The 1st–3rd Armored Amphibian Tractor Battalions provided amphibious fire support during the final approach to the beach, and all saw combat. The Marines also employed similarly equipped Army amphibian tractor and amphibian tank battalions.

The 1st and 2nd Aviation Engineer Battalions were formed in 1943 as FMF troops. Lightly equipped, they were intended to be air-lifted onto islands to repair captured airfields. They were provided with heavier equipment and redesignated separate engineer battalions (to differentiate them from the 1st and 2nd (divisional) Engineer Battalions) on 1 June 1944. They remained FMF troops to serve with IIIAC and VAC respectively. Both were deactivated in 1946.

A wide variety of additional separate units were assigned to FMFPac. These were normally reassigned to amphibious corps and Marine divisions as operations required. They included: replacement battalions and drafts (over 100 were formed); provisional Marine companies and detachments (FMF base security units); 1st–3rd Military Police Battalions[1]; 1st–6th Joint Assault Signal Companies[2]; 1st–6th Amphibian Truck Companies[2]; 1st and 2nd Bomb Disposal Companies[1]; 1st–5th Separate Medical Companies; 1st and 2nd Separate Topographical Companies[1]; 1st–5th Provisional Rocket Detachments[2]; 1st–7th War Dog Platoons[2]; 1st–6th Separate Wire Platoons, 1st–5th Separate Radio Intelligence Platoons; and 1st and 2nd Laundry Companies (reorganised into 1st–8th Separate Laundry Platoons in 1944).

## Service Command, Fleet Marine Force, Pacific

Logistical support of the FMFPac and its far-flung units was of critical importance. The difficulties of providing across-the-beach logistics on a hostile shore were formidable, to say the least. This key command was formed as the Administrative Command, FMFPac on 11 June 1944 from the VAC Administrative Command. It was redesignated

---

[1] The 1st was habitually assigned to IIIAC and the 2nd to VAC.
[2] Made organic to divisions in 1945.

# MARINE UNIFORMS

*A 2nd MarDiv company command post in Garapan, Saipan. The company commander, second from left, speaks on an EE-8 field telephone while the man to the right uses an SCR-536 'handi-talki'.*

Supply Service, FMFPac in August 1944 and then Service Command, FMFPac on 1 June 1945.

The units assigned to the Service Command, and scattered across the Pacific at island bases or in general support of combat operations, included: 1st–4th Service and Supply Battalions; 10th–12th and 18th Service Battalions (Provisional), 1st–3rd, 5th, 7th, 8th and 16th Field Depots; 4th and 6th Base Depots; and 1st and 2nd Field Service Commands.

The 7th and 8th Field Depots were redesignated Service Regiments on 1 June 1945 and reorganised to include headquarters and service, motor transport, and supply and maintenance battalions. (The field and base depots were generally organised with one each of headquarters, general supply, engineer, motor transport, ordnance, signal, and military police companies.) A varying number of the Marine Corps' 51 depot and 12 ammunition companies could be attached for additional support; the depots' strength could range from fewer than 300 to almost 2,000 troops. The first of these were formed in early 1943 to provide logistical support to the divisions.

The service and supply battalions provided support to units in the Hawaii area. In early 1945 the 1st Field Service Command was formed in the Marianas to assist with logistical planning and invasion preparations for the 2nd and 3rd MarDivs. The 2nd Field Service Command was formed on Guadalcanal to assist the 1st and 6th MarDivs.

The Marine Corps provided a comparatively sparse, but functional, selection of uniforms. Complaints of some uniforms' poor quality and ill fit were common, and were accounted for by the Corps' notorious frugality; it is often said that the Marines had to be satisfied with obsolete or cast-off Army clothing. While it was true that the Marines often had to wait while other services received new weapons and equipment, this was not the case with uniforms. Very little in the way of Army clothing was used by the Marines. Most was of unique design, and manufactured at its own Philadelphia Quartermaster Depot of Supplies, established in 1880. The Uniform Regulations of 21 May 1937, with amendments, saw the Corps through World War II.

The Marines employed a number of standard uniform colours. Dress blues had a deep dark blue coat and light blue trousers. The winter service uniform was forest green, originally known as 'field green'. This was a deep, warm green – more green in shade than the brownish-olive drab (OD) used on some items. Khaki was a light tan colour, while uniforms and equipment described as 'tan' were more brown. Field uniforms were sage green, a greyish-green (more green than grey) which rapidly faded to bluish-green and then pale green with repeated washing and exposure. Leather belts, shoes, gloves and service cap visors were made of cordovan; described as 'chocolate' or 'nut brown', it appeared almost black. It had replaced tan leather in 1922 as it went well with blues, greens and khakis. Dark bronze metal insignia and buttons adorned service uniforms. The official Marine Corps colours were scarlet and gold, adopted on 18 April 1925, and used extensively on insignia and unit colours.

The Marines had four basic uniforms: the distinctive 'blues', the forest green winter service, the khaki summer service, and utilities; officers also had a white dress uniform similar in design to blues. These were supplemented by various components to provide different uniform classes. Of these uniforms, it is the faded green 'utilities', or 'dungarees', by which Marines were most readily identified. Perhaps Col.

*Left: Mounted on 1 ton trucks, the 1st Provisional Rocket Detachment of 4.5 in. T45 launchers fires on Japanese positions on Saipan. The 4.5 in. M8 rockets had a range of 4,600 yards.*

*Below: A 37 mm M3A1 anti-tank gun crew crouches behind their less than effective shield. The loader holds a canister round. Additional rounds are held in a canvas bag on the ground.*

Allan R. Millett best describes the World War II Marine in his *Semper Fidelis: The History of the Marine Corps:*

'Barely out of his boyhood, often scared and sometimes blindly heroic, he fought and conquered – and created the image of the modern Marine Corps. On his head rests a helmet covered with camouflaged cloth; his light green cotton dungarees with the black USMC globe and anchor on their left pocket are stained and often bloody; his M1 is scratched but clean; his leggings (if he still has them) cover soft brown work shoes; around his waist hangs a cartridge belt carrying two canteens, a first aid packet, and a K-Bar knife. Burned by the tropic sun, numbed by the loss of comrades, sure of his loyalty to the Corps and his platoon, scornful of the Japanese but wary of their suicidal tactics, he squints into the western sun and wonders what island awaits him.'

### Dress and service uniforms

The most distinctive of Marine uniforms is the 'blues'. Since their inception, the Marines have worn blue wool uniforms, but the modern blue uniform was prescribed in 1912 and modifications introduced in 1922 and 1929. The dark blue hip-length coat had a standing collar, epaulettes, and French-style cuff flaps. Enlisted men's coat had no pockets; officer's had pleated breast and skirt patch pockets secured by buttoned flaps. The collar, epaulettes, cuff flaps and front opening were edged with scarlet piping. Seven gilt buttons secured the front closure. The trousers were light blue with 1½ in.-wide scarlet stripes on both seams for warrant officers, company grade officers (lieutenant to captain) and field grade (major to colonel) officers. Generals wore 2 in. stripes and sergeants 1⅛ in. stripes; corporals had the stripe only on the left leg, and privates first class and privates had none. All trousers had front pockets, but only officers' trousers had hip pockets. The issue of blues ceased in early 1942, with the exception of special issues to specific organisations[1].

Three types of belt could be worn with blues. The 2 in.-wide white cloth dress belt had a large, solid rectangular brass buckle. The enlisted cordovan garrison belt, called the 'fair leather belt', was worn with undress blues and had a small, square open-face brass buckle. The cordovan 'Sam Browne' M1935 officer's belt had brass fittings and a strap over the right shoulder; worn with blues and greens, its use ceased in 1943.

The forest green winter service uniform was introduced in 1912. Originally issued with a standing collar, an open roll collar was prescribed in 1926. The

[1] Marine Barracks, Washington; Marine Detachment, London; Marine Band; and Recruiting Service.

coat, or blouse, and trousers were made of kersey wool. The hip-length coat had epaulettes, Marine- (or Polish-) style cuffs, and two belt loops on the back. The breast pockets were pleated, while the large skirt pockets were box style. Both had flaps secured by bronze buttons. Four bronze buttons secured the front opening. The coat was lined with cotton (post-war coats with sateen). Officers' coats were essentially of the same design, but made of 20 oz wool elastique fabric. Officers sometimes used green breeches.

A forest green heavy wool kersey service overcoat was issued as well. It was double-breasted and had two rows of three bronze buttons, epaulettes, marine-cuffs, and front slash pockets. Officers' overcoats were usually made of a fine beaver felt.

The most unique of Marine uniforms was reserved for men discharged due to undesirability. Regulations required that personnel so discharged be provided with a uniform to return home (enlisted men were not allowed to possess civilian clothes). All services provided standard uniforms without insignia, all except the Marines. Called 'Baby Blue Marines', these individuals were provided a light blue version of the winter service uniform and garrison cap. The coat pockets lacked pleats and other refinements, and had plain buttons.

A tan wool long-sleeved shirt was worn in the winter, and a khaki cotton shirt in warmer weather. Service shirts had patch breast pockets secured by buttoned flaps. Shirt buttons were light brown composite material. A tan necktie, or 'field scarf', was worn with both shirts. A brass 'battle pin' held the collars and field scarf in place. An intermediate uniform consisted of the khaki cotton shirt and green wool trousers. The same cordovan garrison belt as worn with the undress blues was used with the greens, until a green wool model was introduced in 1943. The trousers had only front pockets.

When the 1st MarDiv arrived from Guadalcanal in early 1943, it was issued the Australian battle-dress blouse and trousers, because of a shortage of forest green service uniforms. The wool serge waist-length blouse was OD, termed khaki by the Australians. It had pleated patch breast pockets, concealed pocket flap and front closure buttons. Known as the 'Vandegrift jacket', after the division commander, it proved popular. A US-made forest green version was authorised for officers in December 1944 and for enlisted men in August 1945.

*Below: After relentless Japanese night attacks, 2nd MarDiv troops catch much-needed sleep on Tinian. Utility trousers' cuffs quickly became tattered in Tinian's cane fields.*

*Right: An M1 carbine armed Marine assistant machine gunner hauls a belt of .30 cal. ammunition. His M1 steel helmet, with a late type camouflage cover, is worn reversed to improve visibility.*

*The Marine in the foreground is armed with a 12 ga. M1912 riot shotgun with the stock cut down to a pistol grip. A World War I issue 11 pocket grenade carrier is used for the 12 ga. ammunition.*

The Marines have worn khaki since the turn of the century. The khaki summer service uniform consisted of the cotton khaki service shirt and trousers or breeches. A cotton summer service coat was also available. Similar in design to the green wool service coat, the enlisted men's lacked skirt pockets. Its open collar, replacing the standing collar, was introduced in 1928. The coat's issue ceased in 1942.

The wide-crowned service cap was introduced in 1922, replacing the smaller bell crown style that had been worn since 1912. It consisted of a frame on which a white cotton, blue wool, green wool or khaki cotton cover was fitted for wear with the appropriate uniform; both the white and the blue were worn with blues. The visor and chin strap were cordovan leather. Senior officers' visors were decorated with gilt-embroidered oak leaves and acorns, referred to as 'scrambled eggs' – one row for field grade and two for generals – and had a gilt chin-strap. An elaborately embroidered braid quatrefoil adorned officers' crowns. This matched the white cap, but was a shade lighter than the crown's colour on the blue, green and khaki, as was the officer's ribbed cap band (enlisted men's bands were the same colour and material as the crown).

The garrison cap was made both in khaki cotton and in forest green wool. Sage green herringbone twill garrison caps were manufactured under contract in Australia, but saw only limited field use. The Marines were introduced to the garrison cap in World War I when those deployed to Europe were issued Army uniforms. During World War II, garrison, or 'overseas', caps became the common headgear, for the simple fact that there was no room to carry service caps, field hats and tropical helmets in sea bags.

The broad-brimmed field hat was adopted in 1912. This dark OD wool felt 'campaign hat' sported the distinctive 'Montana peak'. The crown's base was encircled by a brown silk band and a thin brown leather nap-strap was normally worn at the base of the crown's front. Officers wore scarlet and gold hat cords with acorns around the crown's base. Issue ceased in 1943, but the hats were sometimes still used in the US.

The pre-war tropical fibre helmet was of the pith helmet style. Covered with khaki or light OD cotton, its interior was green, and it was fitted with a cloth chin strap over the front brim. It fell from general use overseas early in the war, but was issued to recruits undergoing training and to other Stateside personnel.

The footwear worn with all of the above uniforms were highly polished, ankle-high, rough-side-in cordovan service shoes. Prior to and early in the war, a Marine was issued with two pairs, one to be worn in the field. The soles were too thin for rugged use, and many Marines double-soled them. White cotton dress-gloves were worn with blues on formal

*A 22nd Marines M1917A1 heavy machine gun crew fires on Japanese positions north of Agat, Guam. The watercooled M1917A1 was an invaluable fire support weapon.*

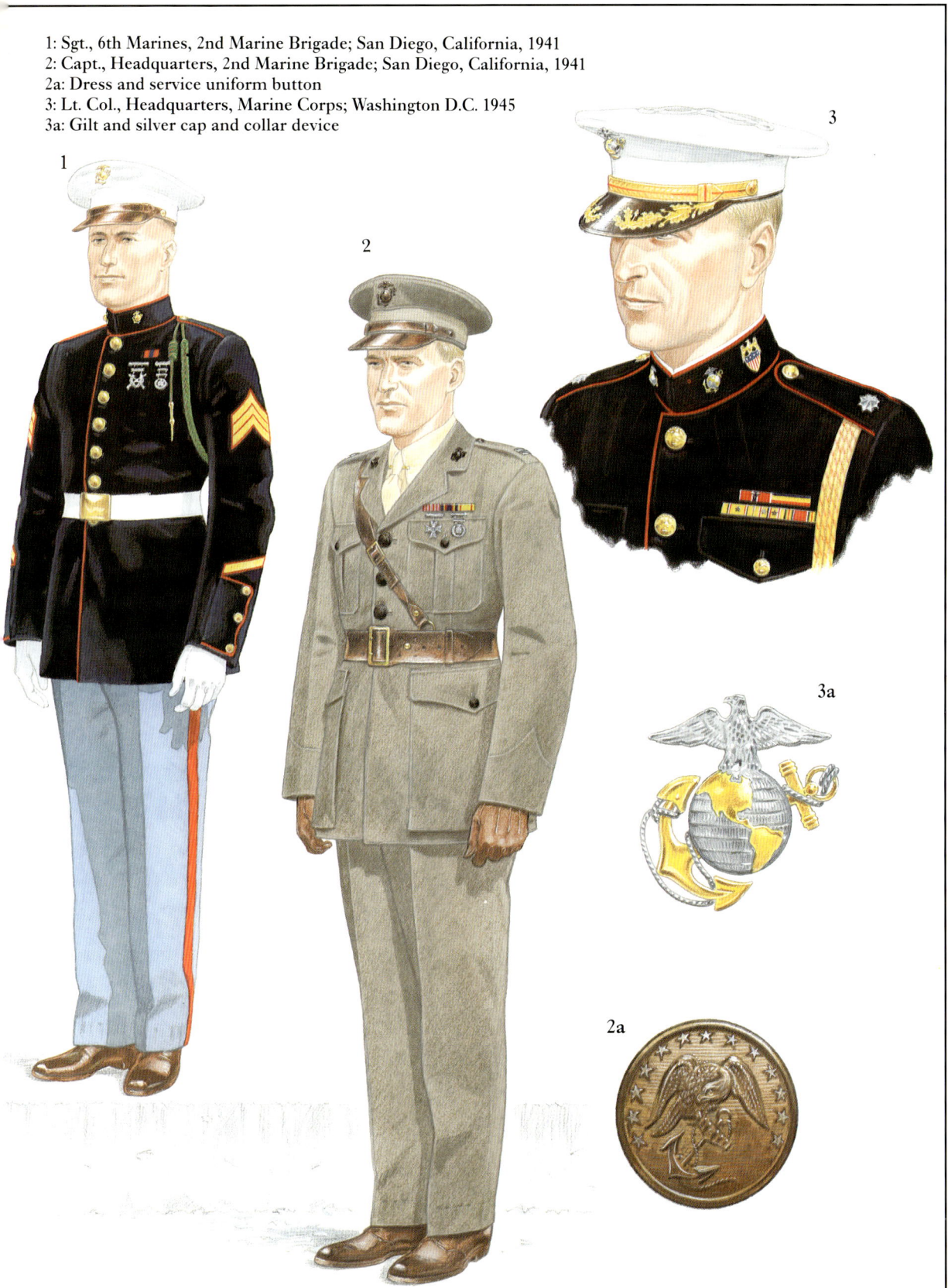

1: Sgt., 6th Marines, 2nd Marine Brigade; San Diego, California, 1941
2: Capt., Headquarters, 2nd Marine Brigade; San Diego, California, 1941
2a: Dress and service uniform button
3: Lt. Col., Headquarters, Marine Corps; Washington D.C. 1945
3a: Gilt and silver cap and collar device

1: Pfc., Company A, 1st Engineer Battalion, 1st Marine Brigade; Iceland, 1942
2: Pfc., 4th Marines (Reinforced); Corregidor, 1942
3: Chief Marine Gunner, Marine Corps Equipment Board; Quantico, Virginia, 1943
4: Capt., Infantry Battalion, Training Centre; New River, North Carolina, 1942

B

1: Cpl., 1st Marines, 1st MarDiv; Guadalcanal, 1942
2: Pfc., 7th Marines, 1st MarDiv; Guadalcanal, 1943
3: Pfc., 9th Marines, 3rd MarDiv; Bougainville, 1943
3a: 3rd MarDiv patch
4: Pfc., 1st Samoan Battalion, USMCR; Pago Pago, 1942

1: Pfc., 2nd Raider Battalion; Makin Island, 1942
1a: FMFPac Raider patch
2: Cpl., 3rd Amphibian Traction Battalion, 3rd MarDiv; Bougainville, 1943
3: Cpl., 3rd Parachute Battalion, IMAC; Bougainville, 1943
4: Staff Sgt., 11th Marines, 1st MarDiv; Australia, 1943
4a: 1st MarDiv patch

1: Pfc., 1st Raider Battalion, 1st Marine Raider Regiment; New Georgia, 1943
2: Pfc., 10th Defense Battalion; Pavuvu Island, 1943
3: Pfc., 8th Marines, 2nd MarDiv; Betio Island, 1943
3a: 2nd MarDiv patch

E

1 and 2: Pfc., 5th Marines, 1st MarDiv; Peleliu, 1944
3: 2nd Lt., 4th Special Weapons Battalion, 4th MarDiv; Roi-Namur, 1944
3a: 4th MarDiv patch
4: Pvt., 4th Marine Ammunition Company, 5th Field Depot; Guam, 1944

1: Demolition Squad, 27th Marines, 5th MarDiv; Iwo Jima, 1945
1a: 5th MarDiv patch

G

1: GySgt., 1st Parachute Battalion; Quantico, Virginia, 1941
2: 1st Lt., 2nd Parachute Battalion; San Diego, California, 1942
2a: IMAC Paramarine patch
3: Pfc., 4th Parachute Battalion; New River, North Carolina, 1943

1: Maj., Headquarters, IIIAC; Okinawa, 1945
1a: IIIAC patch
2: Pfc., 4th Marine War Dog Platoon, FMFPac; Okinawa, 1945
2a: FMFPac War Dog Platoon patch
3: SSgt., Third Fleet Landing Force; Yokosuka, Japan, 1945
3a: Ship's Detachment Patch
4: Sgt., 6th Tank Battalion, 6th MarDiv; Okinawa, 1945
4a: 6th MarDiv patch

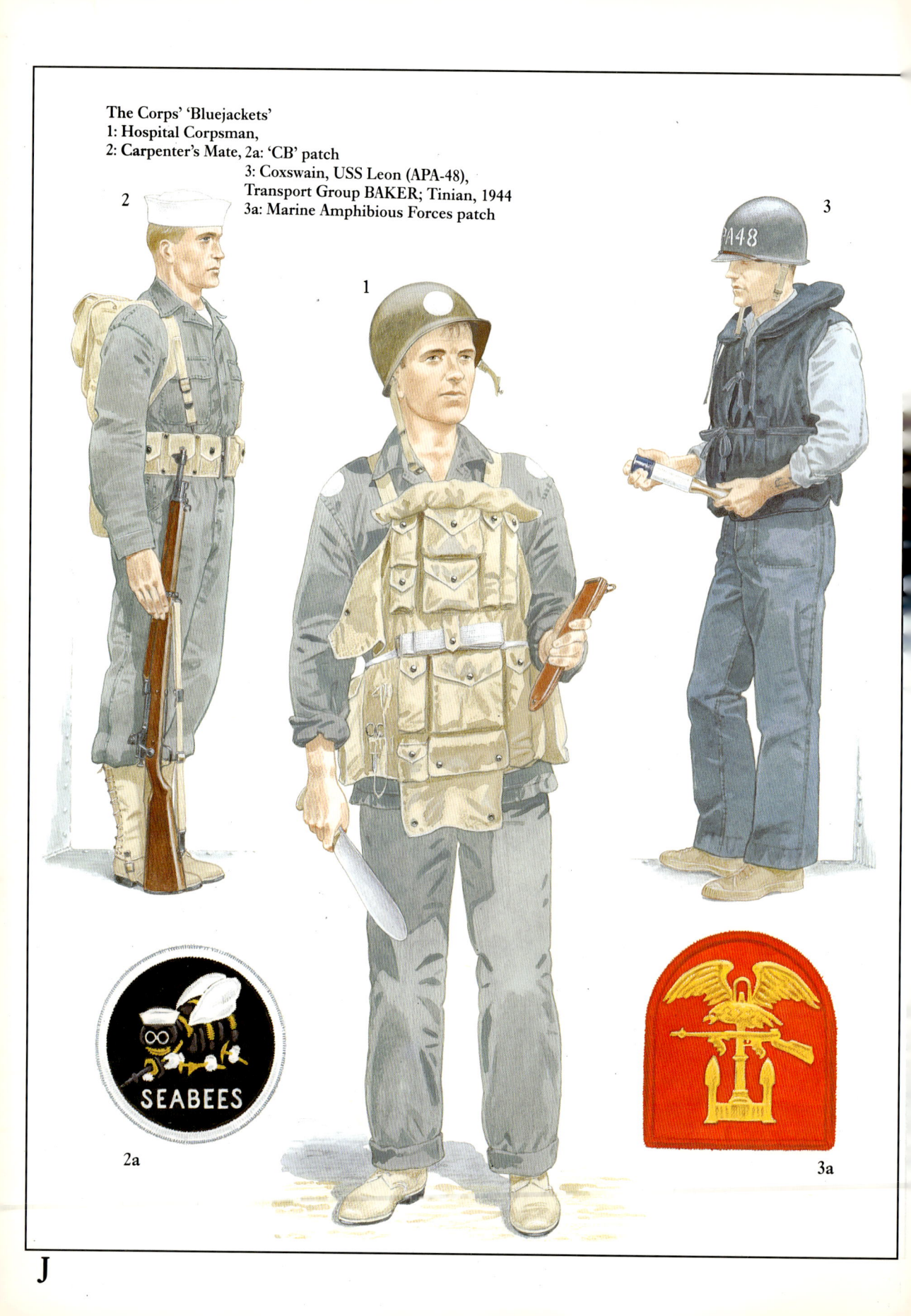

The Corps' 'Bluejackets'
1: Hospital Corpsman,
2: Carpenter's Mate, 2a: 'CB' patch
3: Coxswain, USS Leon (APA-48),
Transport Group BAKER; Tinian, 1944
3a: Marine Amphibious Forces patch

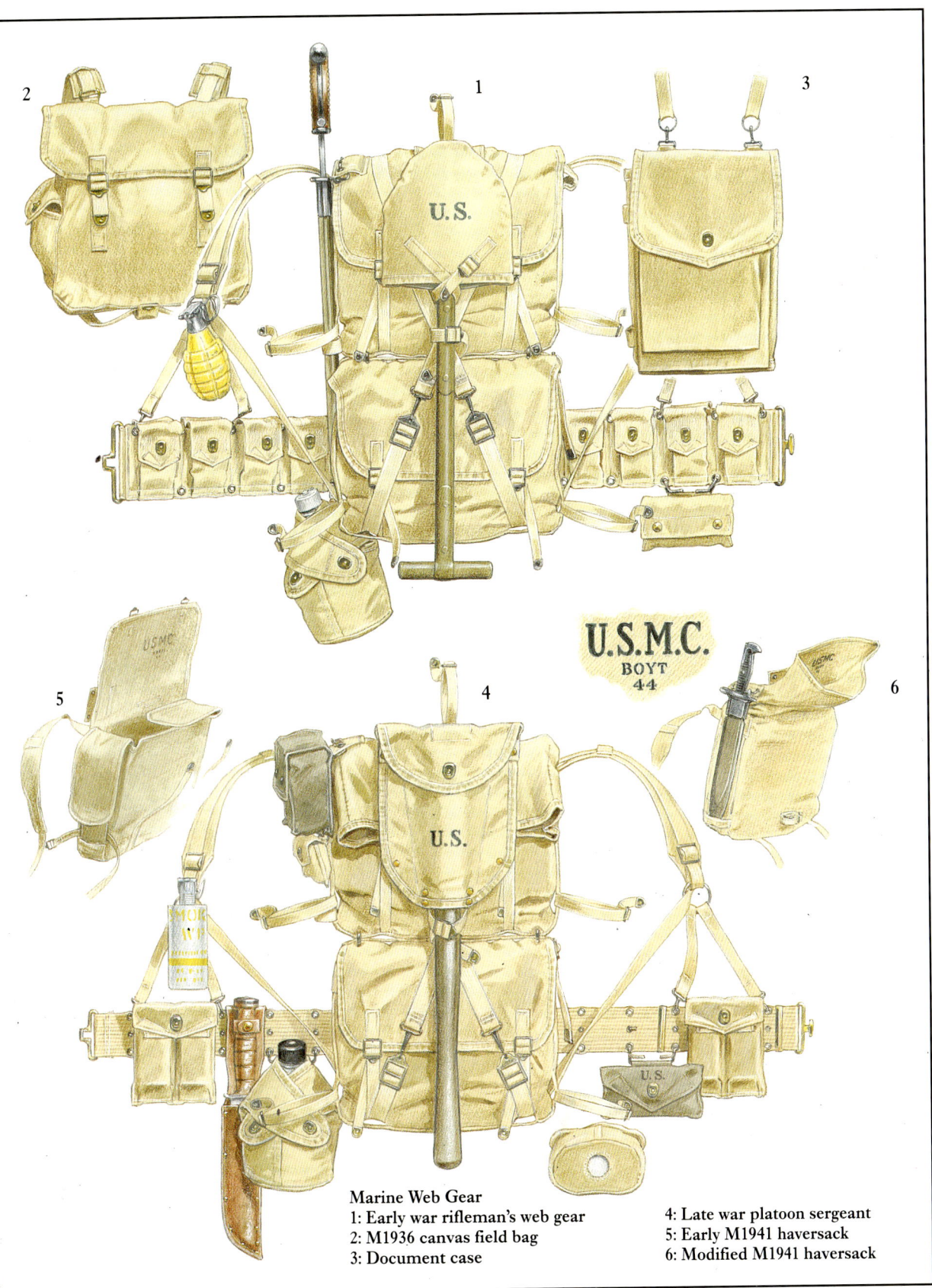

Marine Web Gear
1: Early war rifleman's web gear
2: M1936 canvas field bag
3: Document case
4: Late war platoon sergeant
5: Early M1941 haversack
6: Modified M1941 haversack

K

US Marine Corps Women's Reserve
1: 1st Lt., USMCWR; Marine Barracks, Washington D.C., 1943
2: Cpl., USMCWR; Headquarters Company, Marine Training and Replacement Command; San Diego, California, 1944
3: Pvt., USMCWR, Headquarters, FMFPac; Pearl Harbor, T.H., 1945

occasions, while cordovan leather service gloves were worn with undress blues and greens. A 1¼ in.-wide khaki or tan web belt with a square, open-face blackened brass buckle and belt tip was worn with all trousers including utilities. The blacking was often removed when used with service uniforms.

## Field uniforms

Prior to the introduction of utilities, the wool forest green winter and cotton khaki summer service uniforms were also considered field uniforms. As such, the khakis were without the necktie. Designed more for appearance, they were not practical for field use. The Marines fighting the opening battles at Pearl Harbor, the Philippines, on Guam and on Wake Island wore khakis, while greens were worn in North China and in Iceland.

As field uniforms, khaki or tan canvas field leggings were added to khakis and greens; these had seven eyelets, while the Army's had 16. Ankle-high field service shoes became standard field wear early in the war. These 'Boondockers' were originally adopted as work shoes and were made of light brown rough-side-out leather. They had black rubber or composite soles. To complete the conversion to a field uniform, web field equipment and appropriate headgear were added.

The khaki garrison cap, tropical helmet and field hat were all commonly worn in the field with khakis, as was the M1917A1 helmet, or 'dishpan'. The latter, made of manganese steel, were usually painted forest green, but OD and khaki-painted dishpans were occasionally seen. (The M1917A1 was a modification of the M1917 adopted in 1936, but differed in having improved head pads.) The M1 steel helmet and M1 helmet liner were adopted in 1941, prior to the war, but it was with the dishpan that Marines fought their first battles. By the time of the Guadalcanal landings, the Marines had been fully outfitted with the M1 'steel pot', a helmet made of Hadfield manganese steel. The liner was made of thick, pressed, resin-impregnated duck, and included a web suspension system. Helmet and liner were painted OD. Field expedient burlap and utility cloth helmet covers were first used on Guadalcanal. Some use was made of camouflage nets and burlap stripes fastened to helmets.

Both one- and two-piece dark blue denim utilities were issued from the 1930s as work outfits. In 1941 they began to be replaced by sage green one- and two-piece uniforms made of hardwearing cotton herringbone twill (HBT). These were referred to both as 'utilities' and as 'dungarees'. A black USMC was invariably stencilled above a 'globe and anchor' on the left breast pocket. The two-piece utility suit was first issued on 10 November 1941. It consisted of a shirt (officially a coat) with three flapless patch pockets – two on the skirt and one on the left breast. The front closure was secured by four metal buttons, originally bronze, but changed to blackened steel in August 1942. Early buttons bore a raised 'U.S. MARINE CORPS'. The trousers had front and hip pockets. Originally intended only as a work uniform to be worn over khakis, it was in this outfit that Marines stormed ashore on Guadalcanal.

*An MP of the Military Police Company, 1st Provisional Marine Brigade-guards the brigade command post at Agana, Guam. The M.P. brassard was white on navy blue. This style was used from the 1920s to the 1950s.*

The one-piece mechanic's coveralls were first issued in June 1940 to mechanics and tank crewmen. Parachutists used them from 1942. Tankers often used two-piece utilities or utility trousers and a gray sweat shirt. Coveralls were too hot and had to be almost completely removed when nature called, thus exposing the wearer to marauding insects. Coveralls had flapped, but buttonless, patch pockets on the breasts, hip patch pockets, a long, narrow wrench pocket on the back of the right thigh, and slits on the leg fronts to allow access to trouser pockets.

The HBT utility cap, issued in early 1943, was inspired by a railroad worker's cap. It had a short visor and pleats around the crown, and the 'globe and anchor' was usually stencilled on the front. An HBT utility hat with a floppy brim was also available.

A modified utility uniform was introduced in late 1944. It was little used during the war, and the few that were issued usually ended up on service troops and senior officers. Still of sage green HBT, it incorporated several improvements. The coat had a flap-secured pocket high on the left breast, and large, internal 'map' pockets. An anti-gas flap sealed the inside of the front closure, which was then secured by six metal buttons. The trousers had large bellows cargo pockets with button-secured flaps on the thighs. On the seat was a large, full-width cargo pocket with a three-button flap. A poncho could be carried in this. A redesigned utility cap was issued with this uniform; it incorporated a higher crown and a longer brim. The coat and cap bore the same stencilled insignia as the 1941 versions.

The army olive drab field jacket was adopted by the Marines in 1941. This was a waist-length jacket with the front closure fastened by six or seven plastic buttons and a zipper, with internal slash pockets at the midriff. The outer shell was made of very light OD (actually light tan) water-repellent and wind-resistant cotton poplin lined with flannel. The Army's OD M1943 field jacket also saw limited use with the Marines. This thigh-length coat was made of water-repellent and wind-resistant cotton sateen lined with poplin. The waist was fitted with an internal drawstring. On the chest were flapped bellows pockets, and on the skirt, flapped internal pockets. All plastic buttons were concealed. An OD enlisted man's synthetic raincoat was used in rear areas and the US. It was of simple design, with access slits at the midriff and closed by five plastic buttons.

Issue undershirts and undershorts, or 'skivvies', were made of white cotton. These were often dyed light green and were later manufactured in green. Field socks were a cotton and wool blend and issued in white or, later, in tan.

### Camouflage uniforms

The development of camouflage uniforms was begun by the Army in 1940. Numerous patterns were tested, but what became known as the 'frog' pattern was selected. Designed by Norvell Gillespie, a horticulturist and gardening editor for *Better Homes and Gardens*, it was provided in two spotted, colour combinations for reversible uniforms. The 'green-side' was dark and light greens and dark and light

*A 37 mm anti-tank gun bears the stencilled yellow 1st MarDiv unit marking on its shield. While intended as an AT weapon firing an armour-piercing projectile, the Marines employed it mainly for infantry support using high explosive and canister rounds.*

*Right: Members of a depot company, attached to 1st MarDiv, await orders to move inland from the Peleliu beachhead. White discs were stencilled on their shirt backs for identification purposes.*

browns on a pale green background. The 'brown-side' was dark, medium and light browns, and tan, on khaki. In monochrome photos of the time, the 'brown-side' appears much lighter than the green.

The first camouflage uniform issued to Marines was the Army's 1942 HBT one-piece jungle suit. This was a reversible suit printed with the green and brown patterns and fitted with integral suspenders (often removed). It had pleated breast pockets with buttonless flaps and similar cargo pockets on the front thighs. It presented the same problems as the one-piece mechanic's coveralls: it was too hot, and too heavy when wet. Some Marines cut their own drop-bottom flaps. The jungle suit was issued during the Solomons fighting in mid-1943, but it seems that most wound up in the hands of artillery and service troops, although raiders and parachutists received some.

The Marines adopted their own two-piece camouflage utility uniform in 1943, and it too saw limited use in the Solomons, mainly with raiders and scouts. Similar in design to the 1940 two-piece utility suit, it was made of the same reversible camouflage HBT as the one-piece jungle suit. The coat had flapless patch pockets on the left breast and right skirt, the former printed with the black USMC and 'globe and anchor', and the latter with a button. There were four snaps on the front closure. The trousers had slit front pockets and a patch pocket on the left hip. By the time of the Tarawa and Bougainville operations in late 1943, this uniform was widely issued to infantry units. It was not uncommon for units to wear both 'camies' and sage green utilities, and even for the components to be worn mixed.

*An M1 sub-machine gun armed Marine provides covering fire to advancing 1st MarDiv troops on Peleliu. His equipment includes an M1910 Pick-mattock and five-cell 20-rd. magazine pocket.*

In 1944 the modified camouflage utility uniform was adopted. The coat's patch pockets were replaced by large, deep, internal side-opening breast pockets, secured by a snap and accessible from either side. Similar pockets, secured with four snaps, were fitted on the trousers' fronts, while a large three-snap secured 'butt' pocket was placed on the seat. The coat's front closure was fastened by four metal buttons. The first use of this version was on Saipan in June 1944, and it saw limited use in all subsequent operations; the 1942 version remained in wide use.

The reversible (greens on one side, browns on the other) camouflage helmet cover was issued as a component of the 1942 camouflage uniform. Its introduction heralded a tradition that holds to this day: uniform orders specify 'green-side' or 'brown-side' out. Button hole-like slits were added to covers issued with the 1944 uniform in order to attach camouflage materials. A black 'globe and anchor' was sometimes stencilled on the front. A limited issue cover, commonly known as the 'sniper cover', also saw use. It was non-reversible and made of green camouflage light cotton with a green cloth camouflage retaining-band sewn around the base. It had an integral camouflage-printed mosquito net attached to the bottom edge that could be rolled up inside the helmet.

Other camouflage gear was issued. The Marines had long used a light OD canvas shelter-half. One half was carried by each Marine and when two were

*A Marine gives water to a wounded buddy on Peleliu. A camouflage poncho is secured to the top of his M1941 haversack. The gas mask case on his left hip is used to carry additional gear.*

snapped together, they provided a two-man 'pup tent'. Each Marine carried a three-piece tent pole, a guy line and five wood stakes. In 1943 a reversible camouflage shelter-half began to be issued. The Marines adopted the medium-weight poncho in early 1941. It was made of waterproofed light OD cotton fitted with snaps on the sides. A neck opening slit was provided in the centre and could be closed by means of overlapping flaps secured by a tab and snaps. It was not provided with a hood as Army models. In mid-1943 a reversible camouflage model was issued. Later versions had grommets fitted along the edges to allow it to be used as a shelter. Besides a rain garment, the poncho could be used as a ground cloth or bedroll cover. Individuals sometimes camouflaged utilities, steel helmets and web gear by dabbing on green, brown, or black paint.

## Parachutists' uniforms

Marine parachutists employed a variety of special camouflage uniforms and other unique items. The first item issued was an HBT sage green parachutist coverall designed in 1941. It was copied from the German parachutist smock, as were subsequent models. All smocks could be worn over mechanic's coveralls or utility uniforms. It had mid-thigh length legs, a neck-to-crotch zipper, and large, oval tan canvas-covered leather pads on the forearms. On the sides were large round-bottomed, zipped tan canvas pockets that had leather insert pads; these were to be removed after landing. On the left breast was a flapped, two-snap fastened bellows pocket. USMC was stencilled on the flap with a 'globe and anchor' above it. On the right breast was a larger three-snap bellows pocket. On the back was a large three-snap cargo pocket.

The reversible camouflage parachutist coveralls was adopted in late 1942 and was similar in basic design to the sage green model, but included many refinements. It had large, deep, internal side-opening, three-snap pockets on the chest. A 'poacher's pocket' was provided across the small of the back and was accessible through side-openings secured by flaps, three snaps and a zipper. On the front thighs were two-snap patch pockets. The forearm pads were covered with either OD canvas or camouflage HBT.

The reversible camouflage parachutist utility uniform was designed to be worn with the above camouflage coveralls. It was retained by some former parachutists when absorbed into the 5th MarDiv and worn in combat. Early versions were made of heavy shelter-half material, but most were HBT. The coat had six front closure snaps and two breast pockets with angled openings secured by a single snap. The trousers had internal flapless front pockets on the green side. On the brown side the pockets appeared as patch pockets and were secured by a flap and three snaps. A large cargo pocket was placed on the seat.

*A 1st Marines 81 mm mortar squad leaves the Peleliu front-line after relief by the Army. In 197 hours the 3,200-man regiment suffered 1,672 casualties. Its 1st Battalion lost all its platoon leaders.*

On the green side it was a bellows pocket and it appeared as a patch pocket on the brown side. This side-opening pocket had a three-snap flap on either side.

An improved reversible smock, the modified parachutist camouflage coveralls, was issued in late 1943. The forearm pads were covered with camouflage HBT. There were internal pockets on both breasts and the front legs, each secured by a single snap. It retained the 'poacher's pocket' across the back. The sage green and both camouflage smocks were used only during Stateside training.

A forest green wool jump helmet was used until 1941. This tight-fitting skull cap included an integral throat strap. More commonly used was the A-7 summer flying helmet made of chamois-lined dark brown horsehide with a hard leather chin-cup. It was worn under a standard M1 steel helmet and liner.

Three types of jump boots were used: high-top rough-side-in cordovan boots were initially issued; a high-top version of the light brown rough-side-out leather boondockers saw limited use; and Army issue 'Corcoran' dark brown jump boots were also used. The latter had capped toes, but Marine boots had no caps.

### Further reading

While scores of books are found on the Corps' combat exploits, few discuss its uniforms, insignia and organisation. In these areas, the following are recommended: Jim Moran, *U.S. Marine Corps Uniforms & Equipment in World War II*, Windrow & Greene Ltd (1992); Bert L. Campbell, *Marine Badges & Insignia of the World*, Brandford Press, (1983); Gordon L. Rottman, *U.S. Marine Corps Order of Battle 1941–47*, Brown Mouse Publishing (1995); Radix Associates, 2314 Cheshire Ln, Houston, Texas 77018-4023, USA.

# THE PLATES

### A1: Sgt., 6th Marines, 2nd Marine Brigade; San Diego, California, 1941

Blues were the most distinctive of Marine uniforms and prescribed in two classes, dress and undress. Officers wore the M1935 'Sam Browne' belt in place of the garrison belt. Officers and staff sergeants and higher were authorised a swagger stick, a practice that quickly fell from use. On the left shoulder is the fourragère ('pogey rope') of the French *Croix de Guerre* awarded to the 5th and 6th Marines in World War I. Legend says the scarlet trouser stripes represent Marine blood shed during the Mexican War storming of Chapultepec (1847), but they were worn from 1798. Rank chevrons are gold on scarlet, as are service stripes; one 'hash mark' represents four years of service. The cap and collar 'globe and anchor' devices are gilt. On the breast are the Expert Rifleman Badge with a Requalification Bar and Basic Badge with two Weapons Qualification Bars. Above the badges is the Marine Corps Good Conduct Ribbon.

### A2: Capt., Headquarters, 2nd Marine Brigade; San Diego, California, 1941

The forest green winter service uniform is worn with the 'Sam Browne' belt. Bronze cap and collar 'globe and anchor' devices are worn on greens by all ranks. A different style, but no less traditional, eagle and anchor device adorn dress and service uniform buttons *(2a)*. This design has been used since 1804 and is the oldest military insignia in continuous use in the United States. The ribbons are (from left to right) the Second Nicaraguan Campaign, Yangtze Service

*Artillery men of the 11th Marines haul a 75 mm pack howitzer up a ridge with block and tackle to fire into the Japanese-held 'Death Valley'. Peleliu proved to be the most rugged island encountered by the Marines . . . to date.*

*Left: Marines of the 5th MarDiv rush up the stepped black volcanic sand of Iwo Jima as seen from this landing craft eye view, 1945. A backpacked 'walki-talki' radio can be seen in the lower left.*

*Below: 'Coed', an M4A3 Sherman medium tank of the 4th Tank Battalion, awaits a fire support mission. The sandbags in front protected the crew sleeping position. The hull sides are sided with 2 in. thick wood planks to ward off Japanese hand-emplaced Type 99 magnetic charges.*

(1937–38 Shanghai duty), and China Service; beneath them are the Sharpshooter Rifleman and Basic Qualification Badges. Officers do not wear service stripes.

### A3: Lt.Col., Headquarters, Marine Corps; Washington D.C., 1945

Generals and field grade officers wear gilt oak leaves and acorns on their service cap's visor as well as a gilt chin-strap. The embroidered braid quatrefoil can be seen on the cap's crown. The tradition of the quatrefoil has it origins in the Corps' beginnings, when Marine officers affixed black cord crosses atop their caps in order to be recognised by sharpshooters in the rigging; it was formally adopted in 1859. Officers wear gilt and silver cap and collar devices (3a). This four-star general's aide-de-camp is identified by a gold and scarlet shoulder aiguillette and distinctive collar badges. Aide-de-camps' ranks are progressively higher with each star the general possessed: brigadier generals have lieutenants while full generals rate a lieutenant colonel. They also rated one enlisted orderly per star. The ribbons are the Bronze Star with 'V' Device (for Valor), Navy Presidential Unit Citation with Bronze Battle Star (one for each additional action for which the unit was cited), American Defense Service with Bronze Battle Star, Asiatic-Pacific Theater with Silver and Bronze Battle Stars (a Silver Star equates to five Bronze), and World War II Victory Medal.

### B1: Pfc., Company A, 1st Engineer Battalion, 1st Marine Brigade; Iceland, 1942

The forest green winter service uniform and overcoat doubled as a field uniform in the Icelandic winter. This was supplemented with a forest green wool winter cap with brown fur ear-flaps and bill (previously used in North China). A bronze 'globe and anchor' collar device was affixed to a red backing on the upturned bill. Mustard-coloured wool shirts, wool underwear, heavy wool socks and black rubber overshoes completed the outfit; the trousers were tucked into the tops of the white socks. Hip-length drab canvas, sheepskin-lined coats were rush purchased from Sears Roebuck, as were canvas and rubber foul-weather outfits. The British 79th Division, also garrisoning the island, invited the brigade to wear its 'Polar Bear' patch as a sign of unity. It was accepted and worn on both shoulders in British style. The patches, or 'shoulder marks', as the British called them, were mirrored, so that the polar bear would face forward. The brigade wore the patch with pride until it rejoined the 2nd MarDiv in California. This engineer is outfitted with scrubbed and Blancoed[1] web gear comprising an M1923 cartridge belt (ten pockets with two five-round clips each), M1924 first aid pouch, M1910 canteen and cover, M1905 bayonet and M1910 scabbard, M1910 entrenching tool, ND Mk III gas mask (ND-Navy Diaphragm) and M1928 backpack. His rifle is a Springfield M1903.

### B2: Pfc., 4th Marines (Reinforced); Corregidor, 1942

Khakis were employed as the field uniform until Guadalcanal, when utilities became the combat uniform of choice. The M1917A1 'dishpan' helmet was painted Marine forest green. Although not an official practice, they were often drilled to attach a bronze service cap 'globe and anchor'. This machine gunner is armed with a Lewis Mk 6 Mod 1 machine gun and M1911 pistol. The carrying bag holds a 47-round drum. Besides the khaki M1928 backpack, the Marines also had a forest green version with khaki straps and edge binding.

### B3: Chief Marine Gunner, Marine Corps Equipment Board; Quantico, Virginia, 1943

The chief Marine gunner was a chief warrant officer (CWO) grade designating ordnance specialist. Their rank insignia was a flaming grenade worn on the collars, and a medium blue and gold bar on the shoulder straps. Marine gunners did not wear the bars. In December 1943 CWOs were redesignated commissioned warrant officers, but were still addressed as 'Chief'. A bronze 'globe and anchor' is worn on the tropical fibre helmet. In 1943 bronze-colour devices and buttons were introduced to conserve materials critical to the war effort. Impressed with the Japanese 50 mm 'knee mortar', the Marines searched for a similar weapon. One candidate was the 60 mm T20 mortar. It was fired by a prone gunner at ranges up to 200 yards. While 100 T20s were tested in combat, it was not standardised.

[1] Blanco was a webbing cleaner issued in powder or cake form.

*An 81 mm mortar squad blasts Mt. Suribachi, Iwo Jima, as the 28th Marines advance towards the volcano's base. Emplaced in a bomb crater reinforced by sand-filled ammunition cases, the mortar bears a backup white-painted aiming line on its tube.*

### B4: Capt., Infantry Battalion, Training Centre; New River, North Carolina, 1942

This company commander wears the OD wool felt field hat with the officer's scarlet and gold hat cords. Drill instructors (DI) and rifle teams continued to wear the 'campaign hat' after its general issue ceased in 1943. They were occasionally used in the Pacific, generally in a somewhat more battered condition.

### C1: Cpl., 1st Marines, 1st MarDiv; Guadalcanal, 1942

The two-piece utility suit soon became the standard field uniform. The black stencilled USMC and 'globe and anchor' adorned the left breast on virtually all field uniforms. The M1 'steel pot' had completely replaced the 'dishpan'. Field leggings and boonbockers remained the standard footwear for the war's duration. The venerable '03 Springfield' still armed riflemen, but the M1 rifle was soon to replace it. The wartime tan Marine web gear had begun to be issued.

### C2: Pfc., 7th Marines, 1st MarDiv; Guadalcanal, 1943

Assistant automatic riflemen were armed with M1 carbines. This necessitated the use of a pistol belt and two-cell magazine pockets for the 15-round magazines. They were also issued with three-pocket BAR

*Left: After the famous flag raising (actually the second raising) on Mt. Suribachi, 2nd Battalion, 28th Marines cluster around the site. Three of the six flag raisers died on the island. The flag came from LST 779 and the staff was a Japanese pipe.*

*Below: A 14th Marines 105 mm M2A1 howitzer provides fire support to advancing 4th MarDiv troops on Iwo Jima. The 105 mm served as a general support artillery piece. Most of the crew wear camouflage ponchos to ward off the rain.*

magazine carriers that could hold six 20-round magazines. The utility cap was widely worn in rear areas, and leggings were frequently discarded due to chaffing and because of their increased weight when wet. The cumbersome M1928 backpack was replaced by the M1941 pack system *(Plate K)*. Here the haversack is worn in the marching pack order with an M1910 pick-mattock.

### C3: Pfc., 9th Marines, 3rd MarDiv; Bougainville, 1943

The Army's one-piece jungle suit was the first camouflage uniform issued to the Marines. Scout-observer-sniper teams made use of this hot, cumbersome suit. Many added a burlap helmet cover. This sniper has dabbed green paint on his cover, web gear and leggings in an effort to subdue their light colour. From November 1943 snipers used 'special reference' M1903A1s with a Unertl 8× target scope, which came with a Micarta carrying case. Additional ammunition is carried in a six-pocket bandoleer; each pocket held two five-round clips. While snipers made life difficult for unwary opponents, a key role was counter-sniping. They were usually covered by men armed with Thompsons and BARs. The 3rd MarDiv patch is insert *(3a)*.

### C4: Pfc., 1st Samoan Battalion, USMCR; Pago Pago, 1942

American Samoa, administered by the Navy from 1900–51, became a major base area in 1942 as US forces struggled to halt the Japanese tide. The 1st Samoan Battalion was raised in early 1941 as part of the Marine Corps Reserve, to assist the 7th Defense Battalion by manning guns and patrolling beaches. Led by regular Marine officers and senior NCOs, it was an offspring of the Navy's *Fita-Fita* Guard (Samoan for 'courageous') militia. The Battalion's unquestionably unique uniform, although less 'flamboyant' than the *Fita-Fita*'s, included the traditional *lava-lava* native skirt of scarlet-trimmed khaki. A scarlet-piped khaki garrison cap, white undershirt and scarlet sash completed this one-size-fits-all uniform. A gold 'globe and anchor' adorned a scarlet shield at knee-level, and a smaller version was affixed to the cap. Standard gold on scarlet rank stripes were placed below the *lava-lava*'s shield. M1917A1 helmets were issued.

## D1: Pfc., 2nd Raider Battalion; Makin Island, 1942

On 8 August, 221 raiders of the Battalion's Companies A and B departed Pearl Harbor aboard two submarines. The raiders landed by LCR(2) rubber boat and conducted a reconnaissance in force between 17 and 18 August. Although the raiders lost 30 men, the operation cost the Japanese two troop transports, two aircraft, fuel stores and a radio station. Japanese reinforcements destined for Guadalcanal were subsequently diverted to Makin. Prior to the operation, the raiders were directed to turn in a set of khakis, which were returned to them dyed black. Most wore tennis shoes on the raid. Two hundred Thompson M1928A1 submachine guns were issued to a raider battalion. The Marines were introduced to the Thompson M1921 in 1922 while guarding mail trains after a rash of robberies (which ceased after the Marines took over). Five 20-round magazines were carried in the magazine pocket, the same as used with the Riesing submachine gun. One of the best known of raider weapons was the 'Gung Ho'[1] knife. The Collins No. 18 knife had a 9 in. blade and either a black bakelite or green bone grip. The FMFPac Raider patch is insert *(1a)*.

## D2: Cpl., 3rd Amphibian Traction Battalion, 3rd MarDiv; Bougainville, 1943

Amtrac and tank crewmen often wore one-piece mechanic's coveralls. Rank chevrons were sometimes stenciled (or crudely painted) on field uniforms. This LVT(1) Alligator gunner has donned an M26 life preserver belt. It was also used by Marines aboard landing craft and discarded upon landing. It could be inflated automatically by two $CO_2$ cartridges or orally. Standard LVT(1) armament was an HB-M2 and an M1917A1 machine gun. The latter is

*A 1st MarDiv BAR man fires on counterattacking Japanese, Okinawa, 1945. The weapon's bipod has been removed to reduce its weight. The BAR man wears an M1937 BAR magazine belt.*

carried here in an M7 cover. Amtracs were extremely valuable, being one of the few means available to cross coral reefs surrounding Pacific atolls, but their losses were often heavy: at Tarawa the 2nd Amtrac Battalion assaulted with 125 tractors and lost 90 in 30 hours; the crews suffered 60 per cent casualties.

## D3: Cpl., 3rd Parachute Battalion, IMAC; Bougainville, 1943

The camouflage parachutist utility uniform was worn by the Battalion during its Solomons operations. The Johnson M1941 light machine gun was issued on the basis of three per parachute squad. While actually an automatic rifle, its capabilities were similar to the BAR's, it did have a quick-change barrel and its magazine could be charged while still in the gun, using Springfield five-round stripper clips. Twelve 20-round magazines were carried in the special bag. The rifle cartridge belt was used to carry five-round clips. Other parachutists' weapons included Riesing M55 sub-machine guns and M1A1 carbines. One of three versions of the 'K-Bar' fighting knife, the Camillus Cutlery 1219C, is carried; the three versions were identical but for slight differences in pommel design and blade shape. The other two were the Union Cutlery KA-BAR and the Blade and Tool PAL. The Quartermaster General resisted the K-

---
[1] The phrase 'Gung Ho' was introduced by Lt.Col. Evans Carlson, 2nd Raider Battalion. Chinese for 'work together', it became a Marine byword.

Bar's issue, claiming it was too expensive for the good it would do and that too many Marines would injure themselves; the Commandant overrode that decision.

### D4: Staff Sgt., 11th Marines, 1st MarDiv; Australia, 1943

Australian battle dress was issued to the 1st MarDiv as a substitute for green winter service uniforms which were not available. A khaki shirt and 'field scarf' complete the uniform. The 'Vandegrift jacket' is adorned with the same bronze collar insignia as worn on forest green uniforms. The forest green garrison cap has the same bronze device as worn on the left jacket collar. Officers wear rank insignia on the cap's right front. The 1st MarDiv was one of the first units to adopt a shoulder insignia *(4a)*, although some World War I units had worn patches. What were initially called 'battle blazes' were officially approved on 15 March 1943 for divisions, aircraft wings, and other selected units. They were worn on the left sleeve of overcoats, service coats, field jackets, and shirts worn as an outer garment, but never on utilities. Blue patches were usually sewn over a scarlet backing that followed the insignia's outline to make it more visible on blues, greens and ODs. NCOs with straight 'ties' in their rank insignia ('stripes') were staff specialists rather than 'line' NCOs, who were identified by inverted arches or 'rockers'. Stripes worn on forest green and OD uniforms were forest green on scarlet. From September 1942, rank was worn only on the left sleeve if overseas. Centred on the right sleeve is a Navy Gun Pointer 1st Class distinguishing mark, in Marine colours, indicating service in ships' detachments. Other authorised marks were Gun Captain, Gun Pointer 2nd Class, and Parachute Man. An Excellence in Gunnery 'E' device could be worn 2½ in. above the right cuff. The ribbons are those of the Marine Corps Reserve (four years service) and American Defense Service Medals.

### E1: Pfc., 1st Raider Battalion, 1st Marine Raider Regiment; New Georgia, 1943

The raiders employed a number of unique weapons, among which was the British-designed, Canadian-made .55-cal. Boys Mk I anti-tank rifle. Raiders referred to it as the 'elephant gun'. They also used: M1 rifles, M1 carbines, M1918A2 BARs, M1879 and M1912 shotguns; M1928A1, M1A1 and M55 sub-machine guns; and M1911A1 pistols. He carries M1941 web gear with an M4A1 gas mask in an MIII case. Raiders were among the first units to receive two-piece camouflage utilities and helmet covers. They were initially issued flannel belly bands, an unusual practice from the American viewpoint, to 'protect the [body] surface against the influence of sudden temperature changes'.

### E2: Pfc., 10th Defense Battalion; Pavuvu Island, 1943

Marines tended to 'dress down' to better endure the ceaseless tropical heat and humidity. However, the steel helmet was an essential part of the 'uniform'. This gunner wears a Navy Mk 2 'talker' helmet and sound-powered headset telephone of the type used by shipboard gunners. Early Marine identity discs, or 'dog tags', were oval (later ones were rectangular). While being replaced by 20 mm guns, .50-cal. M2 watercooled anti-aircraft machine guns still equipped defence battalions. The 20 mm had the advantage of a longer range and a high explosive projectile, but the '.50-cal.' had a flatter trajectory due to a lighter bullet backed by a comparatively heavier propellant charge.

### E3: Pfc., 8th Marines, 2nd MarDiv; Betio Island, 1943

Although used earlier, the first widespread use of two-piece camouflage utilities was during the brutal

*A 37 mm AT gun crew off-loads from the rear ramp of an LVT4 'amtrac' on an Okinawa beach. An M1919A4 light machine gun sits in the foreground.*

*A combat loaded 1st MarDiv assistant BAR man rushes across open ground as his unit advances across Okinawa. He carries a BAR magazine belt and rifle ammunition bandoleer.*

and sheer guts. Of the three regiments that assaulted the two-mile-long, 800-yd-wide island and its 4,836 Japanese special naval landing force defenders and Korean construction workers, 1,085 were killed or missing and 2,233 were wounded. Only 17 Japanese and 129 Koreans were taken prisoner. The 2nd MarDiv patch is insert *(3a)*.

### F1 and 2: Pfc., 5th Marines, 1st MarDiv; Peleliu, 1944

The M1918A2 BAR provided the basis for squad firepower. The M1936 BAR belt held two 20-round magazines in each of its six pockets. The BAR's bipod was sometimes removed to reduce weight. It was common for the utility cap to be worn under the steel helmet, on which a late helmet cover with foliage slits is worn. Although not widely used by the Marines, high-top canvas, rubber-soled jungle boots are worn; an ankle-high version was also available. A modified M1941 haversack, with an M1943 folding entrenching tool and camouflage poncho under the flap, is carried. The 18 in. machete was provided tan and OD canvas scabbards. Two canteens were usually carried after the early campaigns. The jungle first aid kit, widely issued after 1943, contained a field dressing, insect repellent, iodine, petrolatum, a tourniquet and bandaids.

November assault on Tarawa Atoll. While reversible, it was seldom worn brown-side out. Also worn is the early helmet cover. This rifleman, crouching in milky white, artillery churned lagoon water, shelters beside the infamous 600-yd pier. He is armed with an M1 rifle, which then equipped the 1st, 2nd and 3rd MarDivs; an M7 grenade launcher is fitted to its muzzle. The old M1923 cartridge belt was still used, but only one eight-round clip could be carried in each pocket. An M1 cleaning rod case is attached to the belt. While the Corps' earlier operations proved their valour and skill beyond doubt, it was the controversial Betio assault that convinced even their strongest critics that they had no peers in tenacity

### F3: 2nd Lt., 4th Special Weapons Battalion, 4th MarDiv; Roi-Namur, 1944

Japanese snipers made it fatal for officers to wear collar rank insignia. Officers were armed with an M1911A1 pistol and M1 carbine, but here a Thompson M1A1 sub-machine gun is preferred. Its 30-round magazines are carries in a three-cell pocket.

*Combat exhausted Marines take a well-deserved rest after prolonged rain-filled, sleepless nights on Okinawa. An M1941 field transport pack assembly lies in the foreground.*

Two seven-round magazines are carried in the pistol magazine pocket. He carried an M1928 document case and an M1936 field bag configured as a backpack *(Plate K2)*, and is also armed with an M3 trench knife in an M6 leather scabbard (M8 was plastic). (The M4 carbine bayonet, adopted in May 1944, was based on the M3.) He holds an SCR-536 'handi-talki'. Individual Marines were issued a printed line-drawing island map for each operation. Its back was ruled to record his chain of command, mission, signal instructions, coordination instructions and so on. The 4th MarDiv patch is insert *(3a)*.

## F4: Pvt., 4th Marine Ammunition Company, 5th Field Depot; Guam, 1944

The Marines strongly resisted the introduction of coloured troops until ordered to do so in June 1942. With the exception of the 51st and 52nd Defense Battalions (neither saw combat), the Corps' 20,000 blacks were relegated to 51 depot and 12 ammunition companies, which were attached to all-white base and field depots. For all practical purposes these companies were stevedore units used to manhandle supplies and ammunition from the beach to the front, leading them sarcastically to call themselves 'Ration Box Commandos'. Company officers and many NCOs were white. A confidential letter of instruction, issued by the Commandant in March 1943, stated that black NCOs would not be of a grade senior to white NCOs, and that few, if any, would be of the same grade. Seven ammunition and 12 depot companies saw limited combat. The 4th Ammo Company, for example, successfully hunted down Japanese stragglers after Guam was declared secure. This 'Montford Point Marine', after the base where blacks were trained, wears a green undershirt, sage green utility hat, and the later type 'dog tag'.

## G1: Demolition Squad, 27th Marines, 5th MarDiv; Iwo Jima, 1945

The 4th and 5th MarDivs formed a provisional 'assault platoon' in each battalion. These were armed with M2-2 flamethrowers, 2.36 in. M1A1 rocket launchers, Mk II hand grenades, and demolitions 'blowtorches, bazookas, pineapples, and corkscrews'. On Iwo, rifle platoons were restructured with two rifle squads and a 'demolition squad'. It had a 'pin-up team' with a bazooka and two BARs, a 'demolition team' of riflemen with bangalore torpedoes and satchel charges, and a 'flamethrower team' with two flamethrowers and protective riflemen. A stencilled 5th MarDiv clothing and equipment marking can be seen on the rocket gunner's back. A 5th MarDiv patch is insert *(1a)*.

## H1: GySgt., 1st Parachute Battalion; Quantico, Virginia, 1941

The first 'Paramarines' wore khakis under the first

*Left: A 155 mm M1 howitzer of one of three Marine 155 mm howitzer artillery battalions to serve on Okinawa fires on Japanese positions. Note the Navy Mk 2 'talker' helmet worn by the artillery man to the breech's left.*

*Right: Marines pause in one of Okinawa's many flattened towns. A K-ration carton is strapped to this rifleman's M1941 haversack along with an M1943 entrenching tool.*

model sage green coveralls. Two-piece utilities soon became more common jump wear, and were often used without the coveralls. The left beast pocket was for D ration cartons (chocolate bars) while the right held field dressings. A cargo pocket on the back held a poncho. The headgear is the short-lived forest green wool jump helmet. The rough-side-in leather jump boots were initially worn. The Johnson M1941 rifle proved to be short-lived, but did see limited combat in the Solomons. Its unique bayonet is attached to the cartridge belt, while a Western Knife Co. W31 utility knife is carried in the coveralls' left side pocket; both edged weapons had leather scabbards.

### H2: 1st Lt., 2nd Parachute Battalion; San Diego, California, 1942.

The reversible camouflage parachutist coveralls were similar to the sage green model, but had modified pockets and pads. It is worn over the camouflage parachutist utility uniform, which influenced the design of the 1944 modified utilities. The A-7 flying helmet is worn under the M1 helmet. The high-top jump boot version of the boonbockers are worn. In combat, the Reising M55 sub-machine gun proved to have serious flaws; some Marines said it was not even a good club! While the Reising was often strapped behind the chest-mounted reserve parachute when jumping, a camouflage leg bag was also issued. A padded camouflage M1910 entrenching tool cover is worn. The IMAC Paramarine patch is insert *(2a)*.

### H3: Pfc., 4th Parachute Battalion; New River, North Carolina, 1943

The modified parachutist camouflage coveralls were issued only to the last parachute battalion activated – the 4th, which was formed from the East Coast Parachute School. An Army-issue M1C parachutist helmet is worn along with Army 'Corcoran' jump boots. He is armed with an M1A1 carbine and Camillus Cutlery Fairbrain commando knife. The carbine will be placed in a tan drop bag and attached under the reserve chest parachute. The NAF 68514 troop parachute's main and reserve had white 28 ft canopies (NAF – Navy Air Factory).

### I1: Maj., Headquarters, IIIAC; Okinawa, 1945

Few modified utility uniforms, with their distinctive cargo pockets, reached combat troops, but they were seen in the rear areas. This staff officer wears miniature rank on his collars; full-size insignia were reserved for dress and service uniforms' shoulder straps. He wears an M7 shoulder holster, designed for the Army Air Forces, with an M1911A1 pistol. On his belt are an M1942 first aid pouch, a pistol magazine pocket, and a lensatic compass pouch. An early type document case is carried at his side. The IIIAC patch is insert *(1a)*.

### I2: Pfc., 4th Marine War Dog Platoon, FMFPac; Okinawa, 1945

War dogs were used as trackers and first employed on Bougainville in 1943. A platoon had 36 scout dogs. The dogs, which the Japanese called 'Devil Dogs', were considered weapons because their powers of smell and hearing enhanced a unit's observation capabilities. Dogs were also used as messengers, with messages placed in a first aid pouch attached to its choke chain or leather collar. Mongrels were considered the most effective, followed by German Shepherds. Dobermans were the most widely used, but were considered too jumpy. The modified camouflage utility uniform was similar in design to the sage green modified utilities, but saw wider use. This dog handler was issued Army canteen covers; Army web gear was widely issued to the Marines by this stage of the war. He is armed with an M1 carbine and PAL 'K-Bar' knife. Each handler carried: 6- and 20-ft leather leashes; a muzzle; a towel; a grooming brush; a third canteen; and cans of dog food or extra C rations. An FMFPac War Dog Platoon patch is insert *(2a)*.

## I3: SSgt., Third Fleet Landing Force; Yokosuka, Japan, 1945

One of the first units to land on Japanese soil was the Third Fleet Landing Force; Headquarters, 2nd and 3rd Battalions were comprised of Marine ships' guard detachments, while 1st Battalion was made up of Navy landing party personnel. The 1941 utilities were still much in use. His Army issue OD field jacket bears the Ship's Detachment Patch *(3a,* also with a black anchor) and forest green on khaki chevrons. He carries the M1941 haversack, knapsack and bedroll (OD shelter-half) in the field transport pack configuration, plus an M3 lightweight gas mask. His duffel, or 'sea bag', is adorned with a custom-painted 'globe and anchor'.

## I4: Sgt., 6th Tank Battalion, 6th MarDiv; Okinawa, 1945

Tankers used the leather M6 anti-crash helmet with integral radio/intercom earphones and all-purpose goggles assembly (issued with clear, green and red lens). An M3 pistol holster is fitted over his mechanic's coveralls. The 6th MarDiv patch is insert *(4a)*.

## J: The Corps' 'Bluejackets'

Several categories of sailors were assigned to or provided direct support to the Marines. Those assigned to the Corps received tactical training from the Marines after their initial naval training. The Navy also provided all the Corps' chaplains while Navy aviators, fire control officers, and signalmen were assigned to amphibious corps headquarters, joint assault signal companies, and landing force air support control units for liaison duties.

## J1: Hospital Corpsman, 2nd Medical Battalion, 2nd MarDiv; Betio Island, 1943

All medical personnel assigned to the Marines were provided by the Navy. In combat they wore Marine utilities. They also wore Marine khaki and forest green uniforms with Navy rank insignia in Marine colours along with the 'globe and anchor'. But when blues were prescribed, they wore standard navy blue jumpers. Marine unit shoulder insignia were approved for Navy personnel serving with Marines in

*A battalion 81 mm mortar crew fires from a textbook firing position. Four-round metal cans had replaced the earlier three-round 'cloverleaf' packaging as a more efficient use of shipping space.*

*A Marine assault team advances up one of Okinawa's innumerable ridges. A BAR man brings up the rear in a position that would allow him to cover the M2-2 flame gunner.*

July 1944. In previous operations, corpsmen had worn Geneva Convention brassards (red cross on white) on the left upper arm and red crosses on helmets. This only provided Japanese snipers with an aiming point. For the Tarawa assault, another means of identification was employed. Plain 3 in. white discs were stencilled on the front and back of the helmet, between the shirt's collar and shoulder seam, and even on trousers' rear hip. Some corpsmen were issued the rather complete S14-075 paratroop first aid kit. Worn on the chest, it dropped open to allow access.

### J2: Carpenter's Mate, 121st Naval Construction Battalion, 20th Engineer Regiment; 4th MarDiv; Saipan, 1944

'Seabees' were recruited from among experienced construction workers specifically for service in these units. Previously the Navy had contracted civilian firms for the construction of overseas advanced bases, but this had led to control problems after the war's outbreak (e.g. most workers on Wake refused to build defences). Approval to form 'CB' units was granted in February 1942. 'CB' officers were assigned to the Navy's Civil Engineer Corps. By V–J Day there were 238,000 Seabees in nine brigades, 31 regiments, and 388 battalions and smaller units. Four battalions were assigned directly to Marine units. Seabees were capable of executing more demanding engineering tasks than Marine engineer battalions, who were assault engineers. They wore standard Navy uniforms and were authorised a 'CB' patch *(2a)* in October 1944 (previously approved in March 1942 to mark equipment). In combat zones Seabees wore mechanic's coveralls, Marine utilities or Navy dungarees. Besides this M1903A3 rifle, Seabees were armed with M1 carbines and M1919A4 machine guns.

### J3: Coxswain, USS Leon (APA-48), Transport Group BAKER; Tinian, 1944

Landing craft crewmen wore the standard Navy work uniform, 'dungarees', as well as utilities. Dungarees included a chambray shirt and denim trousers. An M1 steel helmet (with the ship's number), OD canvas low-quarter safety-sole boat shoes, and kapok life jacket completed the outfit. The most common landing craft was the 36 ft Landing Craft, Vehicle, Personnel (LCVP), of which 23,358 were built. Crewed by four men, they were armed with two M1919A4 machine guns. An LCVP could haul 36 troops, or a 105 mm howitzer, or 37 mm AT gun and a jeep. Three each of red and blue hand-held signal lights (flares) were stowed aboard landing craft for distress signalling. (The red signal's handle was rounded for night identification.) Enlisted men as-

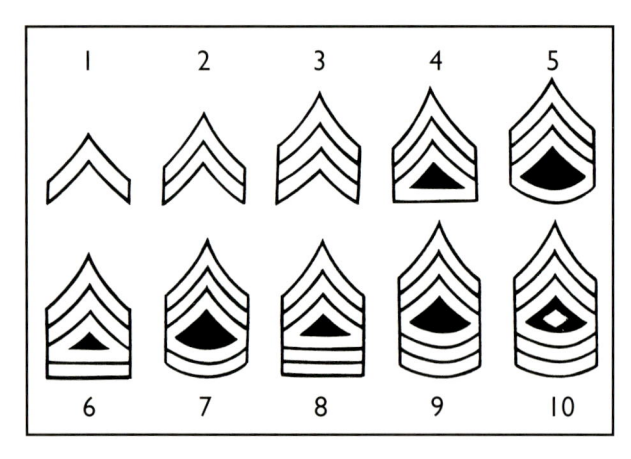

*Enlisted rank insignia. Gold on scarlet backing (for blues), forest green on scarlet (for forest greens), forest green on khaki (for khakis), black stencilled (for field uniforms). Staff NCOs, with straight ties (line NCOs had rockers), included: aviation, mess, music, paymaster, quartermaster, and signals. Line NCOs outranked staffs. Chevrons, rockers, and ties were 3¼ to 3½ in. across and 5/16 to 7/16 in. wide.*
*(1) Private First Class – Grade 6*
*(2) Corporal – Grade 5*
*(3) Sergeant – Grade 4*
*(4) Staff Sergeant – Grade 3*
*(5) Platoon Sergeant – Grade 3*
*(6) Technical Sergeant/ Supply Sergeant/Drum Major – Grade 2*
*(7) Gunnery Sergeant – Grade 2 (First Sergeant prior to 10 February 1943)*
*(8) Master Technical Sergeant/Quartermaster Sergeant/Paymaster Sergeant – Grade 1*
*(9) Master Gunnery Sergeant/Sergeant Major, and First Sergeant after 10 February 1943 – Grade 1*
*(10) First Sergeant – Grade 1 (diamond revived in 1944\*). Note: Private – Grade 7, had no insignia.*
*\* Diamond could be vertical or horizontal, open or solid.*

signed to the Amphibious Forces were authorised a patch *(3a)* in June 1944 (the Army's similar Amphibian Engineer Patch had a blue backing).

## K: Marine web gear

A Marine's web equipment was commonly called '782 gear', after the form on which he signed for his clothing and equipment. The components were similar to the Army's, but there were numerous unique items. Most Marine gear was made by the Philadelphia Quartermaster Depot or the Hoyt Company. Marine web equipment was predominantly tan, although khaki and, after 1943, OD gear was used.

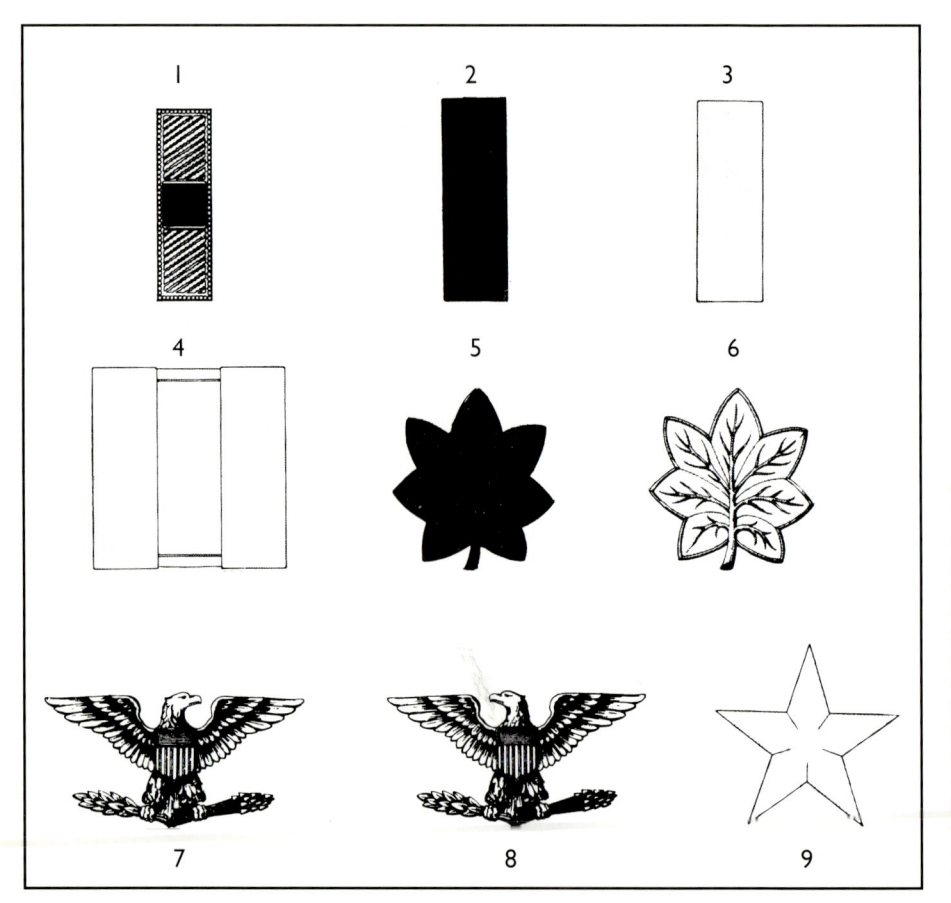

*Officers' rank insignia. All were silver, except 2nd Lt. and Major, which were gold; CWO was gold with a medium blue band.*
*(1) Chief Warrant Officer*
*(2) 2nd Lieutenant*
*(3) 1st Lieutenant*
*(4) Captain*
*(5) Major*
*(6) Lieutenant Colonel*
*(7–8) Colonel (right and left shoulders)*
*(9) Brigadier General (Maj.Gen. – 2 stars, Lt.Gen. – 3 stars, General – 4 stars).*

Most Marine items were marked U.S.M.C., either on the back or under a flap; they were seldom marked U.S. as Army gear was. Marine gear centred around the M1941 pack system, which could be configured in five assemblies: light marching pack (haversack without cartridge belt); marching pack (haversack, cartridge belt, entrenching tool – the normal assault outfit); field marching pack (marching pack with bedroll added); transport pack (haversack, cartridge belt, knapsack); and field transport pack (transport pack with bedroll added). The (upper) haversack contained rations, poncho, underwear, socks, mess kit and toilet kit. The (lower) knapsack held a set of utilities, underwear, and an extra pair of shoes. The bedroll consisted of one or two OD wool blankets (marked USMC) and a mosquito net in a shelter-half with stakes and pole.

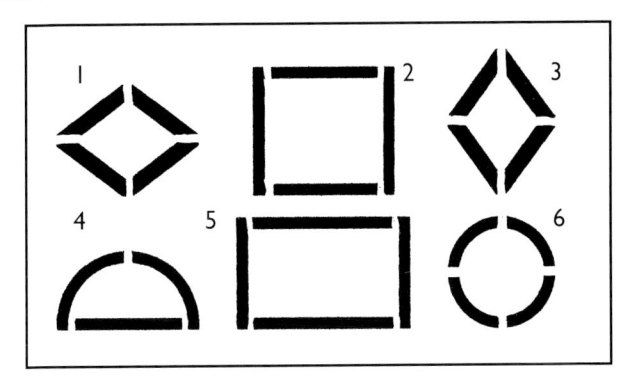

### K1: Early war rifleman's web gear
This assembly includes: an M1941 haversack with M1905 bayonet and M3 plastic scabbard; an M1910 entrenching tool and carrier; M1941 knapsack; M1941 suspenders; M1923 cartridge belt; M1924 first aid pouch; and M1910 canteen with early type cross-flap cover (no drain hole). The Mk II fragmentation grenade bears the early all-yellow colour code.

### K2: M1936 canvas field bag
Known as the 'musette bag', it was issued to officers, non-infantrymen, parachutists and women Marines

*Unit markings. Various sized black stencilled symbols identified unit equipment, clothing, and individual gear. Three or four digit numbers were included within. The numbering system varied, but generally: 1st digit – regiment within division, 2nd digit – battalion (HQ was, identified by 'T', 3rd digit(s) – company; there were exceptions. (1) 1st MarDiv, (2) 2nd MarDiv, (3) 3rd MarDiv, (4) 4th MarDiv, (5) 5th MarDiv, (6) 6th MarDiv.*

in lieu of the M1941 pack system. Its shoulder strap could be configured into double straps to allow it to be carried as a backpack.

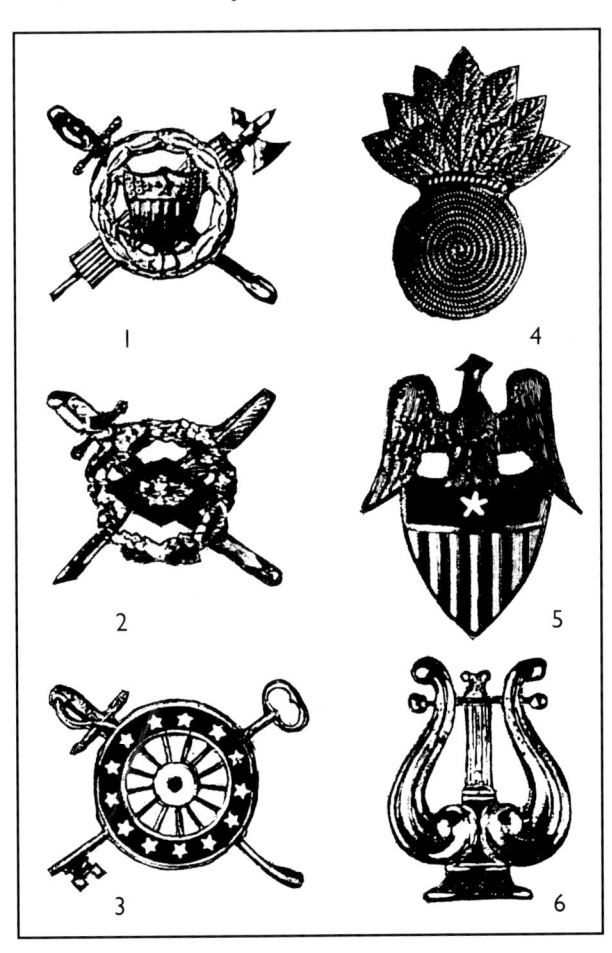

*Specialty insignia. Bronze on greens and khakis, gilt on blues. The first three insignia served as both department devices for specialty officers (worn on coat lapels below the 'globe and anchor', or to the rear of the 'globe and anchor' on standing collars; abolished in 1943) and as rank devices (on shoulder straps above chief warrant officer bar) by CWO Pay Clerks and Quartermaster Clerks. Aide-de-camps wore their device on the collar as did Marine Gunners; Chief Marine Gunners on shoulder strap above CWO bar.
(1) Adjutant and Inspector's Department (gilt)
(2) Paymaster's Department, also Pay Clerk (gilt, red diamond)
(3) Quartermaster's Department, also QM Clerk (gilt, blue wheel)
(4) Marine Gunner (silver)
(5) General's Aide-de-Camp (number of stars equated to the general's) (gilt eagle, red-white-blue shield)
(6) Leader, Marine Band (gilt).*

## K3: Document case
This was issued to officers and staff NCOs to carry maps and message books. While replaced by the M1928 document case *(Plate F3)*, it remained in wide use.

## K4: Late war platoon sergeant
Modified M1941 haversack with jungle first aid kit *(Plate F2)* and M1943 entrenching tool and carrier; modified M1941 knapsack; M1941 suspenders; M1932 pistol belt; two carbine magazine pockets; two canteens with late-type covers (large drain hole); KA-Bar knife; and M1942 first aid pouch with M15 white phosphorus grenade is attached.

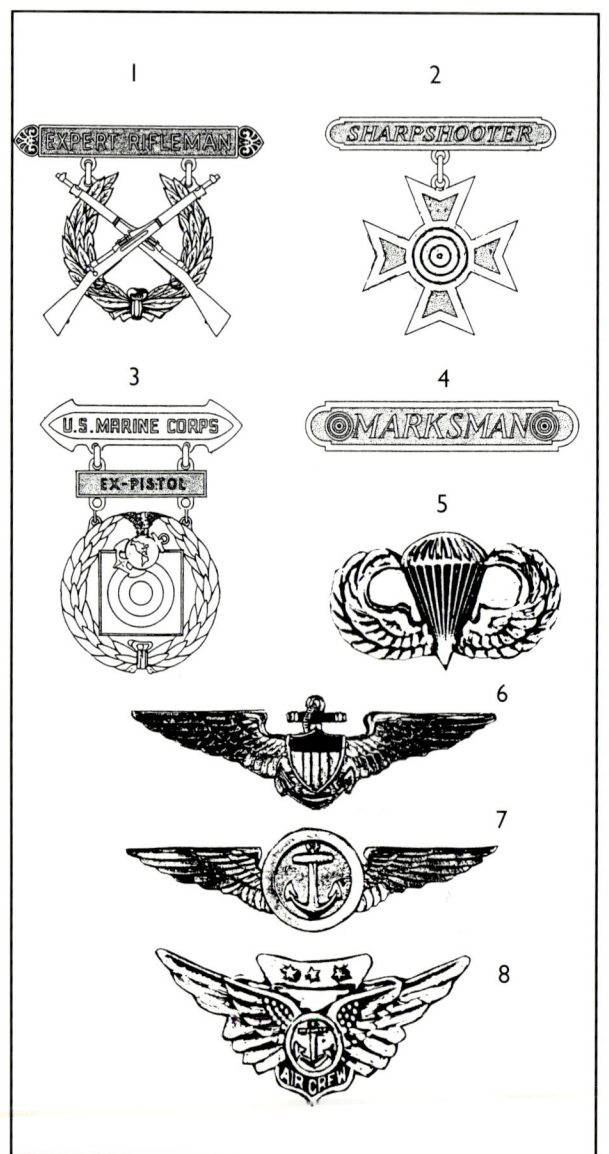

## K5: Early M1941 haversack
Early M1941 haversacks and knapsacks had normal closure flaps and small side flaps. Haversacks had integral shoulder straps.

## K6: Modified M1941 haversack
Modified M1941 haversacks and knapsacks were introduced in 1943 and had a simplified closure system. The pack's body was extended into a throat, which was folded over as a flap. This appeared shorter than early versions' flaps. An M1 bayonet with M7 plastic scabbard, adopted in 1943, is attached.

## L: US Marine Corps Women's Reserve
The USMCWR was formed on 13 February 1943 to relieve manpower shortages (some 300 Marine Reservists [Female] had served in World War I). Women had been assigned to the Marine Corps since late 1942, but were part of the reserve and not a separate branch as in the Army. At the end of 1942 there were 3,100 women in the Marines; none were officers. Female officers were authorised in early 1943, and by mid-1943 there were over 21,300 Women Marines. They served in clerical, administrative and light maintenance assignments in the States. The few deployed overseas were stationed in Hawaii. By VJ-Day there were 18,460 Women Marines. USMCWR uniforms paralleled their male counterparts', although there were no blues. Lacking a catchy title like other services' women, a female reporter coined the term BAM – 'Beautiful American Marines'. It was soon rephrased to mean 'Broad Ass Marines'. The women retaliated by calling the men HAMs – 'Hairy Ass Marines'.

Qualification badges. 1–5 were silver, 6–8 gilt.
(1) Expert Rifleman
(2) Sharpshooter
(3) Marksman
(4) Basic Weapons Qualification (with an Expert Pistol Bar*)
(5) Parachutist
(6) Aviator
(7) Aviation Observer
(8) Air Crewman (stars represent campaign participation).
* Bars were also available for BAR (AUTO-RIFLE), Thompson sub-machine gun (T.S.M.G.), machine gun (MACH.GUN), bayonet, and various artillery pieces. Bar weapons designations were preceded by EX – Expert, SS – Sharpshooter, or MM – Marksman (similar Army bars did not have prefixes).

## L1: 1st Lt., USMCWR; Marine Barracks, Washington D.C., 1943

The USMCWR forest green winter service coat was of the same basic cut as the men's and was worn with a khaki blouse and tie. Officers had a white braid cord on the service cap while enlisted wore scarlet. The six-panel skirt extended 1½ in. below the knee. This uniform could be worn without the coat. A forest green double-breasted trench coat was provided, with a scarlet wool knit scarf. Winter uniform accoutrements included a dark brown leather handbag and light brown leather gloves. Dark brown leather pumps or oxfords and beige stockings were worn with all service uniforms. Women wore the same metal insignia as their male counterparts, but did not wear shoulder patches. 'Montezuma red' lipstick, matching uniform scarlet, was required.

## L2: Cpl., USMCWR; Headquarters Company, Marine Training and Replacement Command; San Diego, California, 1944

The pale green and white striped cotton seersucker summer service uniform was the women's counterpart to men's khakis; its buttons were light green plastic. The scarlet-piped light green summer garrison cap is worn here (officers' were white-piped), but a light green summer dress cap, of the same design as the winter service cap (L1), or an earlier, full-brimmed 'Daisy May' light green summer service hat (replaced by the garrison cap in 1944) could be worn. The summer undress jacket was of the same design, but had long sleeves and only three buttons. An optional white short-sleeved summer uniform was available (five gilt buttons), worn with white pumps. Girdles were mandatory. A light green cloth handbag cover and strap were added to the leather handbag for summer use, as were white cloth gloves. Women's light green on white chevrons worn on summer uniforms (including whites) were smaller than men's, but men's scarlet on forest green stripes were worn on winter service coats.

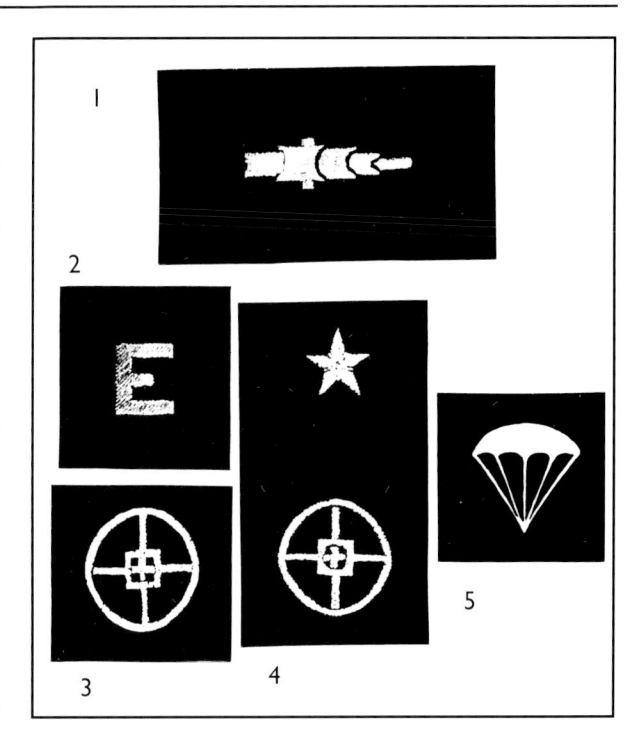

*Navy style distinguishing marks. Available in gold on scarlet (for blues), forest green on scarlet (for greens), and forest green on khaki (for khakis).*

(1) Gun Captain
(2) Excellence in Gunnery (Navy 'E')
(3) Gun Pointer 2nd Class
(4) Gun Pointer 1st Class
(5) Parachute Man.

## L3: Pvt., USMCWR, Headquarters, FMFPac; Pearl Harbor, T.H., 1945

Women were initially issued men's HBT utilities, but in 1944 a woman's cotton twill field uniform was provided. The short-sleeved shirt is worn here along with the sage green 'Daisy May' field hat; a garrison style HBT field cap was also available. The slacks had a bib front and integral suspenders. Women's dark brown field boots complete the outfit. A three-button (brown plastic) long-sleeved shirt, similar to men's utilities, was issued along with an OD field jacket *(Plate I3)*. The Military Police brassard was worn by all Marine MP personnel while on duty.

### Notes sur les planches en couleur

A1 Les 'Blues' étaient les uniformes les plus distinctifs des Marines et existaient en deux catégories, tenue de service et petite tenue. Les officiers portaient la ceinture 'Sam Browne' M1935 au lieu de la ceinture de garnison. Les chevrons et galons sont sur fond écarlate. A2 L'uniforme de service d'hiver vert forêt se porte avec la ceinture 'Sam Browne'. Le motif 'globe et ancre' en bronze sur le képi et le col sont portés sur l'uniforme vert par tous les rangs. Un motif aigle et ancre, de style différent mais non moins traditionnel, décore les boutons des uniformes de campagne et de service (2a). A3 Les généraux et les officiers de campagne portent des feuilles de chênes et glands dorés sur la visière de leur képi de service ainsi qu'une mentonnière dorée. (2b) illustre le motif doré et argent porté sur le képi et le col.

B1 L'uniforme de service d'hiver et le manteau vert forêt étaient également utilisés comme uniforme

### Farbtafeln

A1 Der blaue Farbton war für die Uniformen der Marines am charakteristischsten, und es gab zwei Typen: die Paradeuniform und die Freizeitkleidung. Offiziere trugen anstelle des Garnisonsgürtels den "Sam Browne"-Gürtel M1935. Die Rangwinkel und Streifen der Waffengattung waren gold auf scharlachrot. A2 Die waldgrüne Dienstuniform für den Winter wird mit dem "Sam Browne"-Gürtel getragen. Die Abzeichen "Globus und Anker" in Bronze an der Mütze und am Kragen werden von allen Rangen auf grün getragen. Ein Emblem mit Adler und Anker - zwar unterschiedlichen Stils, doch nicht weniger traditionell -schmückt die Knöpfe der Parade- und Dienstuniform (2a). A3 Generale und Offiziere der Felddienstgrade tragen goldfarbene Eichenblätter und Eicheln auf dem Schirm der Dienstmütze, die außerdem mit einem goldfarbenen Kinnriemen versehen ist. (2b) zeigt das gold- und silberfarbene Mützen- und Kragenabzeichen.

de campagne durant l'hiver d'Islande. Un képi d'hiver en laine vert forêt avec des couvre-oreilles et une visière en fourrure marron venaient s'y ajouter. **B2** le kaki était utilisé comme uniforme de campagne jusqu'à Guadalcanal, lorsque les vêtements de travail furent choisis comme uniforme de combat. **B3** Le chef artilleur des Marines était un 'chief warrant officer' (CWO), grade qui désigne un spécialiste de l'artillerie. Leurs insignes de grade était une grenade en feu portée sur le col et une barre bleu moyen et or sur les épaulettes. **B4** Ce commandant de compagnie porte le calot de combat OD en feutre de laine avec les galons de képi écarlate et or des officiers.

**C1** L'uniforme de travail deux pièces devint rapidement l'uniforme de combat standard. Le sigle USMC noir en transfert et le 'globe et ancre' décoraient la poitrine avec presque tous les uniformes de combat. **C2** Les tirailleurs automatiques assistants étaient armés de carabines M1. L'encombrant paquetage M1928 fut remplacé par le système M1941. **C3** L'uniforme de jungle une pièce de l'armée fut distribué et fut le premier uniforme de camouflage distribué aux Marines. Les équipes éclaireurs-observateurs-tireurs d'élite utilisaient cet uniforme chaud et encombrant. L'écusson 3ème MarDiv est en insert (3a). **C4** Le 1er Bataillon Samoan fut levé début 1941 dans le cadre de la Réserve du Marine Corps pour aider le 7ème bataillon de défense en servant les pièces et patrouillant les plages.

**D1** Cette illustration montre l'uniforme typique d'un Marine du 2ème Bataillon de Raiders durant leur raid sur l'île de Makin, 1942. L'écusson FMFPac Raider est en insert (1a). **D2** Amtrac et l'équipage des chars portaient un bleu de travail de mécanicien. Les chevrons de grade étaient quelquefois peints au stencil (ou à la main) sur les uniformes de combat. **D3** Le bataillon portait l'uniforme de travail de camouflage des parachutistes durant les opérations dans les îles Salomon. La mitraillette Johnson M1941 fut distribuée sur la base de trois unités par équipe de parachutistes. **D4** L'uniforme de combat australien fut distribué à la 1ère MarDiv comme substitut des uniformes d'hiver verts qui n'étaient pas disponibles. Une chemise kaki et un 'foulard de combat' viennent compléter cet uniforme. La 1ère MarDiv fut l'une des premières unités à adopter des épaulettes (4a).

**E1** Les raiders employaient un certain nombre d'armes spécifiques parmi lesquelles le fusil anti-chars cal. 55 de conception britannique et construit au Canada, le Boys Mk 1. Les raiders l'appelaient familièrement 'fusil éléphant'. **E2** Les Marines portaient souvent leur petite tenue pour mieux résister à la chaleur et à l'humidité incessantes des tropiques. Mais le casque d'acier était une partie essentielle de leur 'uniforme'. **E3** Bien que l'uniforme de travail deux pièces ait été utilisé auparavant, il devint très répandu durant le brutal assaut amphibie en novembre sur l'atoll de Tarawa. Bien que réversible, il était rarement porté avec le côté marron à l'extérieur. Le protège-casque est également utilisé. L'écusson de la 2ème MarDiv est en insert (2a).

**F1 et 2** Le M1918AZ BAR formait la base du peloton d'artillerie. La ceinture M1936 contenait deux chargeurs de 20 salves dans chacune de ses six poches. Le bipode du BAR était quelquefois enlevé pour réduire le poids. **F3** A cause des tireurs d'élite japonais, il était fatal pour les officiers de porter des insignes de grade sur leur col. Les officiers étaient armés d'un pistolet M1911A1 et une carabine M1 mais ici l'arme préférée est une mitraillette Thompson M1A1. L'écusson de la MarDiv est en insert (3a). **F4** Les Marines résistèrent à l'introduction de recrues de couleur jusqu'à ce qu'on leur en donne l'ordre en juin 1942. Ce 'Montford Point Marine', ainsi nommé d'après le nom de la base où les noirs étaient entraînés, porte un maillot de corps vert, une casquette de travail vert sauge et la 'dog tag' plus tardif.

**G1** Les 4ème et 5ème MarDiv formaient un 'peloton d'assaut' provisionnel dans chaque bataillon. Ils étaient armés de lance-flammes M2-2, de lance-fusées 2.36 pouces M1A1, de grenades Mk II et bombes de démolition appelés également familièrement 'blowtorches, bazookas, pineapples et corkscrews'. Sur le dos du lanceur de fusées, on remarque la marque peinte au transfert de la 5ème MarDiv. L'écusson de la 5ème MarDiv est en insert (4a).

**H1** Les premiers 'Paramarines' portaient un uniforme kaki sous le premier modèle de bleus de travail vert sauge. L'uniforme de travail deux pièces devint rapidement le plus répandu pour le parachutage et était souvent utilisé sans le bleu de travail. **H2** Les bleus de travail réversibles des parachutistes étaient similaires au modèle vert sauge mais les poches et le paquetage étaient différents. Il est porté sur l'uniforme de travail de camouflage du parachutiste, qui influença la conception des uniformes de travail modifiés en 1944. L'écusson des Paramarines IMAC est en insert (2a). **H3** Les bleus de travail de camouflage modifiés des parachutistes furent uniquement distribués au dernier bataillon de parachutistes mis en service, le 4ème, qui fut constitué à partir des élèves de la East Coast Parachute School.

**I1** Peu d'uniformes de travail modifiés, avec leurs poches bien reconnaissables, arrivèrent jusqu'aux troupes, mais on en voyait dans les arrières. L'écusson IIIAC est en insert (1a). **I2** On utilisait des chiens de combat comme pisteurs. On les utilisa pour la première fois à Bougainville en 1943. Un écusson de Peloton de chiens de combat FMFPac Dog Platoon est en insert (3a). **I3** Une des premières unités à atterrir sur le sol japonais était la Third Fleet Landing Force ; Quartier Général, 2ème et 3ème bataillons étaient composés de détachements de gardes-marines des Marines alors que le 1er bataillon était composé de personnel de débarquement de la Navy. L'écusson du détachement du navire est en insert (3a). **I4** Le personnel des chars utilisait le casque de cuir protecteur M6 avec écouteurs radio/intercom intégrés et lunettes tous usages. L'écusson de la 6ème MarDiv est en insert (4a).

**J1** Tout le personnel médical assigné aux Marines était fourni par la Navy. Au combat, ils portaient l'uniforme de travail des Marines. Ils portaient également l'uniforme kaki et vert forêt des Marines avec les insignes de grade de la Navy dans les couleurs des Marines ainsi que le 'globe et ancre'. **J2** Les 'Seabees' étaient recrutés parmi les ouvriers de construction expérimentés spécifiquement pour servir dans ces unités. Auparavant, la Navy avait signé des contrats avec des sociétés civiles pour la construction de bases avancées à l'étranger, mais ceci entraîna des problèmes de contrôle après le début de la guerre. L'écusson 'CB' autorisé est en insert (2a). **J3** Les hommes d'équipage des bateaux de débarquement portaient l'uniforme de travail standard de la Navy, le 'dungarees' ainsi que l'uniforme de travail kaki. Le 'dungarees' comportait une chemise en chambray et un pantalon en denim. Les recrues affectées aux Forces Amphibies furent autorisées à porter un écusson (3a) en juin 1944.

**K** Les Marines appelaient souvent leur paquetage '782 gear' d'après le formulaire qu'il devait signer pour obtenir son matériel. Les éléments étaient similaires à ceux de l'armée mais il y avait beaucoup d'articles spécifiques.

**L1** Le manteau de service d'hiver vert forêt USMCWR était coupé de la même manière que celui des hommes et se portait avec un chemisier kaki et une cravate. Les officiers avaient une cordelette en passepoil blanc sur le képi de service alors que celui des recrues était rouge. **L2** L'uniforme de service d'été des femmes, en seersucker de coton rayé vert pâle et blanc était l'équivalent de l'uniforme kaki des hommes. **L3** Les femmes reçurent initialement l'uniforme de travail HBT des hommes mais en 1944 on leur fournit un uniforme de combat en twill de coton.

---

**B1** Die waldgrüne Dienstuniform für den Winter und der Mantel dienten auch als Felduniform im isländischen Winter. Die Bekleidung wurde durch eine waldgrüne Wintermütze aus Wolle mit Ohrklappen aus braunem Pelz und einem Schirm ergänzt. **B2** Bis Guadalcanal dienten Khakis als Felduniform, danach wurde der Arbeitsanzug vorzugsweise zum Kampfanzug. **B3** Der erste Schütze der Marines hatte den Rang eines "Chief Warrant Officer (CWO)", was ihn als Geschützspezialisten bezeichnete. Das Rangabzeichen war eine flammende Granate und wurde auf dem Kragen getragen, außerdem hatte man eine mittelblau und goldenen Streifen auf den Schulterklappen. **B4** Dieser Kompaniekommandant trägt die OD-Feldmütze aus Wollfilz mit den scharlachrot-goldenen Abzeichen der Offiziere.

**C1** Der zweiteilige Arbeitsanzug entwickelte sich bald zur standardmäßigen Felduniform. Das schwarz schablonierte USMC und der "Globus und Anker" zierte auf praktisch allen Felduniformen die linke Brust. **C2** Die Geschützhelfer für automatische Waffen waren mit M1-Karabinern ausgestattet. Der sperrige Rucksack M1928 wurde durch das Gepäckstück M1941 ersetzt. **C3** Der einteilige Dschungelanzug der Armee war die erste Tarnuniform, die an die Marines ausgegeben wurde. Die Mannschaften der Späher/Beobachter/Heckenschützen bedienten sich dieses warmen, hinderlichen Anzugs. Das Abzeichen der 3rd MarDiv ist gesondert abgebildet (3a). **C4** Das 1st Samoan Battalion wurde Anfang 1941 als Teil der Marine Corps Reserve zusammengestellt und sollte das 7th Defense Battalion bei der Bedienung von Gewehren und der Patrouille der Strände unterstützen.

**D1** Diese Abbildung zeigt die typische Uniform eines Soldaten der Marines aus dem 2nd Raider Battalion bei dem Überfall auf Makin Island, 1942. Das Abzeichen der FMFPac Raider ist gesondert abgebildet (1a). **D2** Amtrac- und Panzer-Mannschaften trugen oft den einteiligen Overall der Mechaniker. Auf die Felduniform wurden manchmal Rangwinkel schabloniert (oder auch grob aufgemalt). **D3** Beim Unternehmen Solomons trug das Bataillon die Tarnarbeitsuniform der Fallschirmspringer. An jede Fallschirmschwadron wurden jeweils drei leichte Maschinengewehre Johnson M1941 ausgegeben. **D4** Die 1st MarDiv erhielt australische Kampfanzüge als Ersatz für die grüne Winteruniform, die nicht verfügbar war. Die Uniform wurde durch ein khakifarbenes Hemd und einen "Feldschal" vervollständigt. Die 1st MarDiv war eine der ersten Einheiten, die Schulterabzeichen trugen (4a).

**E1** Die "Raiders" bedienten sich einer Reihe einmaliger Waffen, zu denen unter anderem das 0,55-kal. Boys MkI Panzerjägergewehr zählte, das in Großbritannien entworfen und in Kanada hergestellt wurde. Die "Raiders" gaben ihm den Beinamen "Elefantengewehr". **E2** Die Marines neigten eher dazu, sich überflüssiger Kleidung zu entledigen, um die unaufhörliche tropische Hitze und die hohe Luftfeuchtigkeit besser auszuhalten. Der Stahlhelm war jedoch ein wichtiger Bestandteil der "Uniform". **E3** Der schon früher in Verwendung gefunden hatte, wurde der zweiteilige Tarnarbeitsanzug auf breiter Basis erstmals bei dem brutalen Sturmangriff auf das Tarawa Atoll im November eingesetzt. Obgleich er wendbar war, sah man ihn selten mit der braunen Seite nach außen. Außerdem wurde die frühe Helmbezug getragen. Das Abzeichen der 2nd MarDiv ist gesondert abgebildet (2a).

**F1 und 2** Das M1918A2 BAR bildete die Grundlage der Feuerkraft der Schwadron. Der M1936 BAR-Gürtel faßte zwei Magazine mit 20 Runden Munition in jeder seiner sechs Taschen. Das Zweibein des BAR wurde manchmal entfernt, um an Gewicht zu sparen. **F3** Aufgrund der japanischen Heckenschützen war es für Offiziere lebensgefährlich, Rangabzeichen am Kragen zu tragen. Offiziere waren mit einer M1911A1-Pistole und einem M1-Karabiner bewaffnet, hier gab man jedoch einer Thompson M1A1-Maschinenpistole den Vorzug. Das Abzeichen der 4th MarDiv ist gesondert abgebildet (3a). **F4** Die Marines erhoben entschieden Einspruch gegen die Einführung farbiger Soldaten, bis man im Juni 1942 schließlich angeordnet wurde. Dieser Soldat der "Montford Point Marines", die nach dem Lager benannt wurden, in denen Schwarze ausgebildet wurden, trägt ein grünes Unterhemd, einen salbeigrün Arbeitshut und die "Hundemarke" des späteren Typs.

**G1** Die 4th und 5th MarDivs bildeten in jedem Bataillon jeweils einen provisorischen "Sturmangriffszug". Dieser war mit M-2-2 Flammenwerfern, 2,36 in. M1A1-Raketenwerfern, MkII-Handgranaten bewaffnet sowie zur Demolition mit "Lötlampen, Panzerfäusten, 'Ananas' und 'Korkenziehern'". Auf dem Rücken des Raketenschützen sieht man die schablonierte Bekleidungs- und Gerätemarkierung der 5th MarDiv. Das Abzeichen der 5th MarDiv ist gesondert abgebildet (4a).

**H1** Die ersten "Paramarines" trugen Khakis unter den salbeigrünen Einteilern erster Machart. Die zweiteiligen Arbeitsanzüge entwickelten sich schnell zum gängigsten Springeranzug und wurden oft ohne die Einteiler getragen. **H2** Der beidseitig tragbare Tarneinteiler der Fallschirmspringer ähnelte dem salbeigrünen Modell, hatte jedoch abgeänderte Taschen und Polster. Er wird über der Tarnarbeitsuniform der Fallschirmspringer getragen, die das Aussehen der 1944 modifizierten Arbeitsanzüge beeinflußte. Das Abzeichen der IMAC Paramarines ist gesondert abgebildet (2a). **H3** Der modifizierte Tarneinteiler für Fallschirmspringer wurde lediglich an das letzte aktive Fallschirmspringerbataillon ausgegeben, nämlich die 4th, das aus der East Coast Parachute School entstand.

**I1** Nur wenige der modifizierten Arbeitsuniformen mit ihren charakteristischen Frachttaschen erreichten die Kampftruppen, doch sah man sie in den hinteren Reihen. Das Abzeichen der IIIAC ist gesondert abgebildet (1a). **I2** Kriegshunde wurden zur Spurensuche eingesetzt und kamen erstmals 1943 in Bougainville zum Einsatz. Das Abzeichen der FMFPac War Dog Platoon ist gesondert abgebildet (3a). **I3** Eine der ersten Einheiten, die auf japanischem Boden landeten, war die Third Fleet Landing Force; Headquarters, 2nd and 3rd Battalions setzten sich aus Schiffswachabteilungen der Marines zusammen, während das 1st Battalion aus Landungstruppen der Marine bestand. Das Abzeichen der Schiffsabteilung ist gesondert abgebildet (3a). **I4** Auf den Tankern benutzte man den Sturzhelm M6 aus Leder mit eingebautem Funk-/Intercom-Kopfhörer und Mehrzweckschutzbrille. Das Abzeichen der 6th MarDiv ist gesondert abgebildet (4a).

**J1** Alle den Marines überstellten Sanitäter stammten aus der Marine. Im Kampf trugen sie die Arbeitsanzüge der Marines. Außerdem trugen sie die khakifarbenen und grünen Uniformen der Marines mit Rangabzeichen der Marine in den Farben der Marines sowie den "Globus und Anker". **J2** Die "Seabees" ("Meerbienen") wurden speziell für den Dienst in diesen Einheiten aus den Reihen erfahrener Bauarbeiter rekrutiert. Zuvor hatte die Marine für den Bau von Stützpunkten im Ausland zivile Firmen unter Vertrag genommen, doch hatten sich durch diese Vorgehensweise nach Kriegsausbruch Schwierigkeiten bei der Aufrechterhaltung der Ordnung ergeben. Das vorschriftsmäßige Abzeichen der "CB" ist gesondert abgebildet (2a). **J3** Die Mannschaften der Landungsschiffe trugen die standardmäßige Arbeitsuniform der Marine, "groben Arbeitsanzug" sowie den üblichen Arbeitsanzug. Zum groben Arbeitsanzug gehörte ein Chambray-Hemd und Hosen aus Denim. Unteroffiziere und Mannschaften der amphibischen Streitkräfte erhielten im Juni 1944 ein Abzeichen (3a).

**K** Das Gurtzeug der Marines wurde allgemein als "782 gear" bezeichnet und zwar nach dem Formular, das man bei Entgegennahme der Bekleidung und der Ausrüstung unterzeichnete. Die einzelnen Bestandteile der Ausstattung glichen denen der Armee, doch gehörten auch eine Reihe einmaliger Gegenstände dazu.

**L1** Der waldgrüne Winterdienstmantel der USMCWR hatte grundlegend den gleichen Schnitt wie der der Männer und wurde mit einer khakifarbenen Bluse und Krawatte getragen. Offiziere hatten eine weiße Schnur an der Dienstmütze, die Unteroffiziere und Mannschaftsränge hatten scharlachrote. **L2** Die Sommerdienstuniform aus hellgrün und weiß gestreiftem Baumwoll-Seersucker war das Gegenstück der Frauen zu den Khakis der Männer. **L3** Ursprünglich hatte man den weiblichen Kräften die HBT-Arbeitsanzüge der Männer ausgegeben, doch stellte man 1944 eine Felduniform aus Baumwollköper für Frauen zur Verfügung.